DRAWN TO LEAVE

DRAWN TO LEAVE

My family's escape from our homeland

Anna Sagi

First Published in 2018
by Monterey Press
7 Westbourne St
Brunswick VIC 3056
Australia
www.montereypress.com

Copyright © Anna Sagi, 2018

All rights reserved. No part of this publication may be reproduced, stored in a retrieval system or transmitted in any form by any means, electronic, mechanical, photocopying, recording or otherwise, without the prior written permission of the publishers and copyright holders.

Anna Sagi asserts the moral right to be identified as the author of this work.

National Library of Australia

A catalogue record for this book is available from the National Library of Australia

ISBN: 9780648116332 (paperback)

*To my beloved children Andrew,
Leanne and Evette, and my
grandchildren Caitlin and Jake*

ACKNOWLEDGEMENTS

Without the encouragement of my husband Kalman, this book would not have been written. Andrew's help was also invaluable, and there have been many other family members and friends who have encouraged me to record my family's history. I would also like to extend thanks to Jenny Abramov.

Contents

Prologue 1

Part One

Early years 7
Troubles 23

Part Two

Escape 53
Asten Lager 85
Waiting for Dad 99

Part Three

Salzburg 115
Australia 121

Prologue

It was 1949 and I was only five years old. But the experience is etched in my memory as if it were only yesterday.

It was the very early hours of the morning, perhaps two o'clock. My mother and eight of her nine children – including me, the seventh of the nine – were all fast asleep. The youngest of us slept in a front room while the others were at the back of the house. My father and oldest brother, Miro, were in the bakery, preparing bread for the day ahead.

All of a sudden I was jolted awake by a thunderous thumping and banging on the wooden shutters over our bedroom window. Thump, thump, thump! Bang, bang, bang!

In a haze of sleep, it took a few moments to understand that the noise was being made by someone on the street. The noise got louder. There wasn't just one person, but a few. And now they started shouting and calling out to my father.

'Daniel! Daniel! Come out. We want to talk to you.'

Within minutes the whole family was awake and crowded together, shaking with fright in the blackness. The banging and shouting went on and on, but we couldn't see who it was or how many of them there were because all the shutters were down. Of course this meant that they couldn't see inside either.

They thumped the shutters and knocked on the downpipes, and their language got angrier as there was no response from inside.

'I'll just go out and see what they want,' said my father.

Mum pleaded with Dad. 'No, Daniel. Don't. They will harm you, they will beat you up.' In the gloom I could make out the profound fear in my mother's face – I can still see it today. She was shaking like a leaf, which only made the rest of us more frightened. 'Let's just be quiet and pretend no one is here.'

'I'll just open a window and talk to them,' said Dad.

Mum held Dad by the shoulders and looked into his eyes. 'Please don't,' she begged, forcing herself to keep her voice down. 'We don't know who they are. They haven't identified themselves. But whoever comes at this ungodly hour, it is bad news; they are up to no good. For the sake of the children, please listen to me.'

'Open up, Daniel!' the men shouted amongst the banging. The noise seemed to get louder still, as no one answered.

My youngest brother Slavobran (who was always called Branko), just a baby in his cot, started to cry. One of my older sisters picked him up and put a hand over his mouth to quieten him. She gathered up us younger ones and took us down the back, but we still couldn't escape the hullabaloo.

Meanwhile, someone managed to peek out through a gap in a shutter and saw that there were four men out there. There was just enough light on the street to recognise who they were. Two were local policemen, one was a local politician and the other was someone my father knew was a member of UDBA, the Yugoslav State Security Service. They were all holding rifles.

Huddled in the back room with most of my siblings, I understood none of this at the time. I was trapped inside a thunderstorm, with no idea why. It was terrifying, and it seemed to go on forever.

At long last, after what was about an hour but felt like much more, the noise stopped. Perhaps they became convinced no one was home, or perhaps they had just had enough, but the men finally left. The danger had passed, but we were all left extremely agitated and sleepless for the rest of the night.

When the new day broke, it was as if nothing had happened.

My parents told us not to say anything to anyone outside the family about what had happened. No one who came into my father's bakery said anything, even people who lived nearby and must have heard some of the racket. No one wanted to get involved. All that was left was the dread that it would happen again — a dread that stayed with all of us for weeks to come.

My family, circa 1953.
Rear (L to R): Miro (inset), Veronka, Milinka, Ruženka, Daro
Front: Vlado, me, Mum, Branko, Dad, Elenka

Part One

Early years

World War II was coming to an end by the time I was born in 1944, in the country then known as Yugoslavia. My parents called me Anna. At this time in my country, Marshal Josip Tito was taking control after the devastating war in which over a million Yugoslavs had been killed. Amongst rural people like my parents, expectations were high that Tito's communist regime would bring a better life for all. That's what they had been promised.

My father, Daniel, grew up in what is now Croatia. He had eight brothers and the family were very poor. In the early 1920s when he was about fourteen years old, he was sent to an orthodox priest to help him find work. The priest sent him to a book printer to work and learn that trade. When the printer died prematurely, Daniel started an apprenticeship with a baker and, after finishing his training, he moved to the small town of Bački Petrovac to take up a job with Čani's Bakery. It was there that Daniel met a friend of the Čani family, a local Slovàk girl by the name of Maria Palenkàš, and before long he knew that this was the girl he wanted to marry.

Bački Petrovac – often called just Petrovac – is in the state of Serbia but is a majority Slovàk town. Slovàks remain one

Main street of Bački Petrovac in the 1950s

of several minority ethnic groups in the former Yugoslavia, though they had lived in this region for 200 years by the time I was born. The area was so strongly Slovàk that when my father, who was of Serbian background, moved there he was immediately an outsider. He had to work very hard to win over the local community as his customers. He also had to use all his charm to win over Maria's family.

Maria was the youngest of four, the child of a single mother, her father having deserted the family many years earlier. They lived on and worked a farm inherited from Maria's grandfather. When my father asked permission to marry Maria, her mother had no objection but Paul, one of Maria's two brothers, did.

'This is not right. Daniel is not one of us,' said Paul. 'She should marry a Slovàk boy. There are fine young Slovak boys who are interested and willing to marry her.'

When some of the townspeople heard the news they also

voiced disapproval that he was 'stealing' one of the town's favourite girls. 'You can't marry a stranger,' they told Maria. 'What is wrong with our Slovak boys?'

But my grandmother told my mother that Daniel should not be judged on the basis of his nationality and Daniel did get his permission. My parents married at the age of twenty-one. Unfortunately, Paul remained so upset with the idea that he didn't attend the wedding.

The beginning of Daniel and Maria's married life was difficult, as it is with many beginnings. They were as poor as church mice. However, they worked hard and my father started to build a reputation for himself as a kind and honest man. This reputation slowly overcame the doubts of the local people, including a wealthy Jewish family who eventually made him a loan to make a start on his own. My parents bought an old house with a thatched roof, in a good location not far from the town centre. The house was demolished and in its place a bakery was built with an adjoining shop and residence at the back. The business was soon thriving, as was my father's good relationship with the Slovàk people. He even improved his Slovàk language, which endeared him to the locals even more.

By the outbreak of World War II my parents had five children. Those were hard times for everybody. There were shortages of many groceries, including coffee, sugar and yeast, which of course was essential for bread making. People had to improvise and make coffee, for example, from roasted chicory and oats, sugar from sugar beet and raising agent for bread from hops. Sometimes it was necessary to travel from town to town in search of the essentials.

My parents, Maria and Daniel

My mother's mother was a member of the local Nazarene church, and my mother eventually adopted this faith also. The Nazarene church is a relatively small Christian denomination that practices Anabaptist traditions, meaning members are baptised as adults, not infants, and women typically wear a head covering during worship. Nazarenes have a very strong belief in peace and equally strong objection to the weapons of war.

My father had a religious upbringing in the Serbian Orthodox church, but after attending church one day with Mum, in the 1930s, he eventually joined the Nazarenes as well. In their church services there was a lot of singing and there was also a very nice choir that sang in four parts without musical instruments, and Dad really enjoyed this.

So both my parents were strict Christians who held their beliefs very dear. We were raised with traditional Christian values, including following the Ten Commandments, 'Do unto others as you would have them do unto you', 'If someone asks for a shirt, give them your jacket as well'. However, we were not expected to attend church regularly; the Nazarenes don't believe in converting others so it was our individual choice whether to go or not. The biggest effects of religion on my life were probably that I was not supposed to read fiction, especially fairy tales, and some of the kids at school called me 'Faithful' because my parents were religious. Also, we were taught to be extra polite – we visited an aunt once and she had this plate full of beautiful homemade cookies that she offered to us and we all had to say, 'No, thank you,' even while the adults helped themselves. I still regret that to this day.

Religion affected some of my siblings much more than me, especially my eldest brother, Miro. But I'll come back to that.

If there is one thing that was the centre of our lives growing up, it was the bakery. We lived at the back of my father's bakery, coming and going through the shop many times a day. The bakery defined the relationships my siblings and I had with our parents and the way our whole family interacted with our community.

During my younger years I rarely saw my father. He was in the bakery for much of the night and then slept for much of the day. He had assistants, including my eldest brother, Miroslav – always called Miro – for a few years, but the only time he wasn't working in the bakery himself was when he travelled – sometimes for days at a time – to find supplies of firewood. Bački Petrovac was as flat as this kitchen table, with no forests at all, so Dad would need to go away to find wood. The bakery operated six days per week, so Dad had Sunday off except for Sunday evenings, when he would need to prepare the bread for the next day.

Bringing us up was Mum's job, which she did largely single handedly except for some home help occasionally and, later, help from my three older sisters as they grew up. Milinka, the fourth eldest of us, was seven years older than me and became like another mother to me. The older sisters used to bath and dress us younger kids when we were very young. Ruženka could be a bit of a grouch when we didn't go along with her

Daniel's bakery – the Serbian spelling of his name is Damjan. (He is on the left)

efforts to dress us up nicely, while Veronka was very fashion conscious and put ribbons in our hair and even used a hot iron sometimes to curl our hair for photos.

The bakery's shop faced onto the street and, as I said, was connected to the house. This meant that Mum could do housework at the quieter times, only coming out to the shop if she heard the bell ring on the door. When we got home from school or being out to play the bell rang too, and we would quickly have to yell out, 'It's only me!' so she wouldn't be interrupted for nothing.

Like most bakeries, the busiest time in the shop was first thing in the morning. My mother worked in there and so did my big sisters when they were old enough. Bread was baked into large two-kilogram and five-kilogram loaves, then customers would buy it by weight. If they wanted one kilogram, for instance, a piece would be cut off a larger loaf, using a huge and very sharp knife. One of the reasons why Dad won the trust of the community was that he was always honest with these measurements. His scales were tested by the authorities for accuracy and he never interfered with them, unlike many other places.

Many local farmers didn't have much money, so Dad would

Daniel and an assistant

exchange bread for flour: one kilogram of bread for one kilogram of flour. Farmers would take their wheat to the nearby mill and have it ground into flour, then bring the flour to the bakery. Again Dad was honest, usually giving a bit more bread to allow for the weight lost during baking. People didn't need to weigh their flour before they came – it would be weighed in the shop, though this did cause some problems at times. More than once gypsies would hide an egg or two inside their flour. Eggs are denser than flour, so this meant Dad got less flour for the amount of bread he gave them. Another time there were some gypsies in town who mixed small pebbles into their flour. The worst was the day some gypsies mixed lime into their flour. That was disastrous because you couldn't tell the difference, and when the bags were emptied into the hopper with all the other flour, it all got mixed together. All the bread that night came out flat and had to be thrown away, leaving Dad with a big loss and customers without any bread.

There was a blackboard on the wall to write orders for different products, like long loaves or wholemeal bread (most of the bread was white) or rolls called *keefla* that were knotted a bit like a pretzel.

The shop also sold other products from time to time. Sometimes Dad might find something interesting on his travels that he thought his customers would like – even a wood-fired kitchen stove one time – and he would bring them back to sell. He also kept some bees as a hobby, so we would sell the honey through the shop. Mum and Dad would also make sauerkraut and sell that. Everything added up to make ends meet.

Dad never got rich from his bakery but there was always enough bread for the customers and enough food on our table. We always had plenty of bread, of course, and home-made bacon or ham. We had a mixture of chicory and roasted barley to drink instead of coffee, which was too expensive. And we would put lard on our bread instead of butter, which was kept for cakes on special occasions. Sometimes in the morning, before we went to school, Dad would slice hot bread just out of the oven. We would spread lard on it, a sprinkle of salt and red paprika and then Dad would put it back in to the oven. That was our toast, and it was lovely. Something else that was expensive to buy was eggs, so they were mostly used to make noodles or cakes – not for breakfast.

There was also always enough for people who couldn't afford to buy bread. A little old lady would come in to the bakery and say, 'Daniel, I've got no money and nothing to eat'. Dad would always give someone like that some bread, or extend them credit just because he trusted people to repay him. I remember one Saturday – it was market day, when people came to town from all around to buy and sell their produce – and a total stranger walked into the shop to ask for a glass of water. I was in the shop this time and Dad asked me to take him into the kitchen and give him some water and something to eat. I might have given him some chicory too. It was this kind-heartedness that helped to build Dad's reputation.

The bakery was a real community centre too. Because the oven was always hot, some of the local women would bring cookies in to bake during the day, when there was no bread to cook. They might pay a little to do this. There was one day when a lady brought some biscuits in and Mum agreed to watch them while the lady did her errands. Then Mum forgot the cookies and they burnt. She quickly got the ingredients together and made another batch. I was told that when the war ended they even used the oven to roast a piglet for the celebration.

Over time my parents, and even the rest of us, actually became quite well known, even in Slovàk areas quite a long way from home, because Dad was such an important and respected person in the community and because of my parents' involvement in their church. 'You're a Vasic,' people would say to me, even many years later and on the other side of the world. 'I knew your parents.'

My early life as a child in Bački Petrovac was simple but enjoyable. We had plenty of freedom to play, and there were lots of people to play with between my brothers and sisters – the younger ones around my age – and friends from school and around the neighbourhood (even though my mother was selective about who she wanted us to play with).

Maybe the only thing that was a bit different for us was that, because of my parents' strict religious values, we were discouraged from listening to the radio, going to the cinema or reading novels. The last one was the hardest for me because I loved books – I still love books. One time we were asked to read a fairytale story at school and then write an essay about it, but my parents refused to buy me such a book because the fairytale stories are not true. Luckily my older sister Veronka, who had the keys to the till in the bakery, gave me enough money to buy the book myself. I would put it inside a school book so when Mum walked into my room all she would see was the school book and think that I was still a good girl!

Mostly we just made up our own games.

There was a shed near our house that my father built, with its floor raised off the ground. Dad intended to store his firewood in there to keep it dry, but in the end it was too much hassle to lug the wood up and down the ramps. Instead the shed became a giant cubby house where we could play endless make-believe games, like pretending we were on a boat to America or Canada. I played a lot with my brother Vlado, who was two years older than me, and his friends. Sometimes that included soccer when they let me – when they needed an extra player. 'The babba can play,' they would say, using a word that really means old woman or grandmother, but they meant as 'weakling'.

Sometimes we would find some mischief to get up to. We had pigs in our backyard that were fed corn but also needed green grass, so my mother would send my brothers to the road outside town to collect some grass from beside the road. Normally they would take some of their mates with them, and sometimes they would let us girls go with them too. There were fields of poppies beside the road and their seeds were great for a snack. The boys would tell us girls to stand on the road and lookout for any ranger or farmer, and to give a special whistle if we saw someone coming. Then they would take a pocket knife into the field and shake the poppy heads to see if they were ready for harvesting. They would cut off the good heads and stuff them into their shirts until they could hold no more. We would then hide in the bushes, cut open the heads and eat the seeds. It was great fun, though the next day we would all suffer from great constipation.

Sundays were always a big day in our town, almost like a weekly Christmas. We wouldn't see anyone heading to the fields with farming implements over their shoulders; there were no horse carriages on the road. Instead there would be little old ladies heading to church with their bibles in their hands. Mum and Dad went to church too, and even though we didn't always do that, we usually dressed up in nice clothes. Sometimes the older girls stayed at home to prepare the meal, and on other days we younger kids would get together with our cousins and walk around. A favourite place to go was the cemetery, which was a bit macabre, especially on Sundays. Not only did we see some nice plants at the cemetery and the roses that people would plant there, but we would amuse ourselves reading the different inscriptions on the tombstones. Sometimes we would pick wild blackberries too, though Mum didn't like us doing that as it could be considered work.

Throughout the day we would hear the peal of the church bells, though that happened on other days too. The bells were used to communicate funerals and weddings – different patterns of ringing for each. They rang at different times of the day too, like when it was time for school to start and at the end of the school day. We also had a town crier. When the local government needed to announce something, a large drum was pounded and everybody would come out onto the street. The town crier would wait till there was a large enough group of people and then make his announcement.

Our winters were cold, often with heavy snow, and so more

time was spent indoors. Sometimes aunts and uncles would come over. The women would bring their spinning wheels with them – they were of the upright variety and easily carried – and would sit around spinning hemp or wool into yarn while the men stood around talking and chewing on pumpkin seeds. My favourite times were when we were allowed to stay up late and listen as they shared ghost stories – I still love a good ghost story. Another winter task was weaving, using the spun yarn. Some women had a loom set up in their home on which they would make cloth for tea towels, table cloths, bedding and so on. It was fascinating to watch the way they could build a pattern into the fabric, the shuttle (we called it a 'boat') flying back and forth.

Mum also made clothes using fabric that my father found on his travels, or from a Jewish lady who would drop in with rolls and rolls of material at cheaper prices than Mum could buy in the shops.

Another memory I have of winter was my father encouraging my older sisters to help with the shovelling of the snow. We didn't have arranged marriages in our society, but Dad thought that if his daughters were seen working hard, then the fathers of eligible boys would be impressed. If a boy was interested in marrying a girl, his father would approach her father. Her father would then ask the girl if she was interested, and if she was the couple would be allowed to go out courting for three months.

A highlight of spring was the return of the birds, especially the magnificent storks. I loved to watch the male storks repairing

An image of the storks from an old children's book

their huge nests, which usually were left from the previous year. Eventually the mother stork would arrive to lay her eggs and then sit on them to incubate them, the father bringing her food of frogs, lizards and so on. After hatching, the parents brought food for the nestlings, making a loud 'click, click' sound as they fed them while standing on one leg. Whenever we children in the town saw this behaviour we would stop for a minute and stand on one leg – doing that would bring us good luck. As the chicks got bigger they would stand up on the edge of the nest before they learnt to fly, eventually ready to fly away before the next winter.

Our house was very self-sufficient – Mum bought as little as possible from the shops. In spring and summer when the fruits came in she would make jam from plums and other fruits. She also preserved cherries. Mum made cakes with poppy seeds, and *pirohy*, which is like a noodle pastry, rolled out flat and fairly thin and then dotted with jam or a paste of ground poppy seeds. Another sheet of pastry was placed on top and then she would use a special little wheel to run along between the dots of jam and seal the edges, forming little parcels. She then cut the parcels into squares and dropped them into boiling water to cook. We loved these! She also made filo pastry, which was amazing to watch. In the centre of a large table with a cloth on it, she would place a piece of dough about the size of a dinner plate. Mum would put a small amount of melted lard on the pastry, then, walking around and around the table, she would very gradually stretch and thin the pastry. Eventually it would cover the whole table, even hanging over the edges, and, except on the very edge, it became so thin you could see through it. She would cut off that thick edge, add a filling like cottage cheese (my favourite) and, using the table cloth underneath to support the fragile pastry, she would throw it in a special way to roll it up. The final product was made from many layers of this very thin pastry. Finally it was cut into lengths, put on to trays and baked, then drizzled with melted lard. Other fillings were cabbage (Dad's favourite) or grated potatoes.

So that was my life for many years. Family, the bakery, adventures. School, friends and plaited hair. We weren't well off, but we had everything we needed. It was a good life.

Troubles

During the war, when the Germans occupied Yugoslavia, my father was forced onto a truck with a large number of Jewish people. They were all told they were going to a work camp. Just before the truck left, a Hungarian man objected. He pointed to my father and said to the guards, 'This man should not be on the truck. He is a Serb, and he is married to a Slovàk girl'. My father was told to get off and so avoided being sent to what he learnt later was a concentration camp. Many of the people sent on that truck and others like it never returned.

Many years later, I was standing in the shop one day, not doing much except listening in to the adult conversations between the customers and my parents. A lady entered the shop in a very upset state. She told my father that her husband had been arrested and was facing death by firing squad for being a war criminal.

Immediately Dad took off his apron. 'Who is the judge?' he asked the lady. 'I will talk to him.'

My father knew this lady. She was the wife of the Hungarian man who had spoken up all those years ago. It was this man who was now under arrest for war crimes.

Dad went straight to the nearby city of Novi Sad, the main

city in our region. He found the judge and told his story about how this man had almost certainly saved his life during the war. The Hungarian man was innocent. He was not a criminal, he was a hero.

The judge thanked Dad for coming but said he was sorry, the decision was out of his hands. The man had already been convicted. Dad returned home feeling very bad.

Very early the next morning – at about 4 am – the judge appeared at our bakery to talk to Dad. We had no phone, so travelling to Bački Petrovac was the only way the judge could contact him.

'Daniel, I have not been able to sleep,' said the judge. 'I understand that an innocent man has been convicted and sentenced to death. But I have worked out a way he might be saved. You must go and find his wife and tell her to appeal the court's decision. When she does that, we'll call you as a witness and you can tell your story.'

And that's what happened. The wife appealed, Dad told the court his story and the Hungarian man was acquitted. Now they had saved each other's lives.

I was friends with the daughter of this man and remember being very sad a little while later when she told me they were moving away, to an area where there were more Hungarians. I never knew whether they chose to do this or were forced to, as some were.

Another time I went to Novi Sad with Dad to visit a Jewish family. They had given my father a box during the war, just before they were sent away to a 'work camp' themselves. They told Dad, 'If one of us or any of our family return, give this back to them if you want to'. The box was put into a back room and forgotten about, though one of my older sisters looked into it at one point and said it was full of silver cutlery. Thankfully they did return and on this occasion I went with Dad to see them and return their cutlery. All I remember was how beautiful their house was.

As we left that house I asked my father why we weren't friends with these people.

He said, 'Because we are being watched, and it would not be approved of for us to be friends with this family'.

At the age of about ten, I had no idea what he meant by that.

By 1949, the people of our area were becoming more and more disillusioned and discouraged by Tito's communist government. It was becoming harder to access simple things like milk. The better life that people had been led to expect after the war was now seen as just empty promises.

In order to deal with their public relations problem, the communists started putting pressure on prominent citizens to join the party. That's why they started leaning on my father to join up. He was a well-loved and respected community member and a successful business owner. If people like him joined the party, it would set a good precedent and encourage others to join also.

The government were also trying to establish farming collectives to replace private ownership. They called these *zadruga,* using a Slavic word for a different type of family-based collective farming that had been common in the 1800s. Dairy farming was already heading this way, with a government-owned business buying all the milk from the farmers – they were forbidden to sell their milk to anyone else – and then distributing it from a central place. The farmers could only earn a wage set by the government. This soon led to long queues of people waiting to buy milk. Despite this, they wanted to do the same with the bakeries, the government taking over ownership of the three bakeries in Bački Petrovac.

At the start they made big promises. 'We'll make you a millionaire.' 'We'll make sure your children get the best education.' 'We'll make you the manager of the *zadruga*.' When my father didn't respond to these promises, they started to get more pushy – like turning up in the middle of the night and bashing on our windows.

Unfortunately for the communists, my father had no interest in joining them. It went completely against his Nazarene religion to be associated with any group or organisation that did not believe in God. Nazarenes are also pacifists, and the communists had a reputation for using violence to achieve their goals. Dad heard of plenty of others like him who just joined the party to make their lives easier, and it worked. But my father would not turn his back on his religion.

My younger siblings and I understood none of this, of course. We were too young. It wasn't until the night of the bashing on the windows that we had any idea that there was trouble, though even then we were too young to understand what was really going on. For weeks after that we worried that it would happen again, but things went quiet and eventually we just went back to our normal lives.

Each night after dinner, Dad went into the bakery to start the bread for the next day. He would combine flour, water and yeast to let them ferment before the next step of the breadmaking procedure.

One night, soon after he had gone to start this job, a messenger arrived from the council with a note asking Dad to come to the council office at 8 o'clock that evening.

'Well, that is strange,' said Mum. 'It is after normal office hours. What do they want with you at this hour? I'm sure it can wait till tomorrow. You should ignore it and go in the morning.'

'It's okay,' said Dad. 'I will run over and see what they want.'

He washed all the flour off his face and arms and headed for the door.

'Take your jacket with you,' said Mum. 'It will get cool later.'

'I won't need it – I'll be back soon.'

An hour later Dad hadn't returned and Mum was looking uneasy. Her feeling of foreboding increased as more time went on and still there was no sign of him. Hours passed and Mum was starting to panic. Finally she decided to go to the council offices to see what was holding Dad up for so long. She asked my older sisters to help Miro in the bakery and to tuck us young ones into bed, then she headed out into the dimly lit streets, carrying Dad's jacket, as it was now quite cool.

Later on she told us what happened.

As she was approaching the council building it was all in darkness except for one window that was bright with light. *That is where Daniel must be*, she thought. The front door to the building was slightly ajar so she went into the dark lobby, then fumbled her way through the darker corridors until finally she saw a bar of light underneath one of the office doors. Stopping outside that door she could hear voices, but not clearly enough to know whose they were. She knocked, then tried to open the door but without success, as it was locked. Suddenly all went quiet, and the light under the door went out. Mum knocked harder, but there was still no answer ... no noise at all.

Eventually Mum called out. 'I know you have my husband here. Open the door and let him come home,' she said.

There was no answer.

'What do you want with him?' she asked. 'Let him come home. It is not right what you are doing, keeping my husband here at this late hour. I know you are here. I saw the light before you turned it off. It is obvious that you are up to no good – what do you want with him?'

Silence.

'Haven't you caused us enough trouble yet?' Mum continued. 'Let Daniel come home and leave us alone to live our life in peace.'

She waited, but still there was no response.

'Please do not hurt him. Our children need him. Who will provide for our children if you harm him? You are breaking the law. There is no law that permits this to be done to good citizens.'

Defeated, with tears in her eyes, Mum decided she had no choice but to go home without Dad.

'At least let him have his jacket. It is cold,' she said, leaving the jacket on the floor outside the door.

On her return home, Mum told us that Dad was being held against his will. The sad reality was sinking in that her husband had been kidnapped. It was all too much for her. She went into her bedroom, sat on the bed and wept uncontrollably. It was hard for we young children to understand, so we just huddled around her and cried with her, unable to find any words to comfort her. My older siblings went into the bakery, doing what they could to make sure that the bread would be ready in the morning. After a while, when Mum composed herself and wiped her tears away, she rolled her sleeves up and went to help in the bakery too. With a combined effort, everything was started and at two in the morning Mum and my older sisters went to bed to get some sleep so they could attend the shop. My oldest brother, Miro, and Dad's assistant stayed up to finish the baking.

Next morning there was bread as usual, our customers totally unaware of the drama the family was experiencing.

At 8 o'clock, as soon as the council offices opened, Mum went back to look for Dad. She went from department to department searching for answers, but everyone she came across said they knew nothing. This only added to her anguish.

'What do you mean, you know nothing about it?' she said, over and over. 'Someone in here requested a meeting with him last night. The notice was delivered by one of your messengers.

Yet now you are pretending to not know anything about it. I don't believe you.'

She told anyone who would listen that she would not give up … she was going to find her husband.

'My husband is a hard-working, law-obeying man, minding his own business. He came here at the request of someone in this office, and now he has disappeared and no one knows anything about it. This is outrageous, you better not harm him. He has dependent children to raise.'

She got no help. If anyone knew anything, they were keeping their mouths shut for fear of getting into trouble.

Holding back tears, Mum left the council building and went to the police station to report Dad missing and ask them to help find him. She found very little sympathy there either, though at least she wasn't surprised by that. She knew perfectly well that the police would have been in on whatever had happened.

Back at home, having made no progress, Mum's brother Paul tried to comfort her.

'He will come home, I'm sure. They will not hurt him,' said Paul.

We heard nothing for a few days until eventually an elderly man came into the shop. He said he was a council employee and asked to speak to Mum privately.

'I am in the communist party,' he told her. 'It gets me a job; it is my bread and butter. But I am not one of them. I do not like what they stand for. I do not approve of this communism, and I can no longer tolerate seeing what they're doing to you and your family. I know where your husband is, and I will tell you if you promise never to reveal where you got the information from. If you betray me, I will be in grave trouble and will lose my job, my livelihood.'

Mum agreed, of course. 'You have my word of honour. I will never reveal the information or anything about this conversation.'

The man told Mum that Dad was in a police lock-up in the nearby town of Futog.

Mum expressed deep gratitude for his kindness and his understanding of her troubles.

The next day she went to Futog by train. It was a small, quiet town, just fourteen kilometres from Bački Petrovac. Once there, she went straight to the police station.

'I know you are holding my husband, Daniel Vasic, here in the lock-up. I insist that you release him.'

The policeman denied this, and wanted to know who had told her that Dad was there. And of course Mum didn't tell him.

'I know that you are holding my husband here, locked up, for no apparent reason,' she repeated.

'I don't know what you are talking about Mrs Vasic,' said the policeman.

Ignoring his denials, Mum went on. 'Let my husband come home,' she said vehemently.

But once again, no amount of pleading would help.

Finally Mum was reduced to tears. Helpless, frustrated and exhausted, she had no other choice but to return home, not knowing where to turn next. She was filled with fear, without any knowledge of what the future held. Family and friends could not console her.

But she could not give up. Every day she continued with her complaints of the injustice being perpetrated against law-abiding citizens.

A week passed. Business in the bakery was running smoothly with my brother Miro and his assistant producing bread during the night, and in the morning Mum serving customers in the shop, with the help of my older siblings.

After dinner one evening, two of my younger siblings and I were playing with some neighbourhood children on the street outside our home when I noticed the figure of a man approaching. He was a way away, but despite my shortsightedness there was something familiar about the way this person was walking, so I stopped to watch him attentively. Finally he was close enough that my eyes could make out some detail.

'Dad! Dad is coming home', I shouted. Everyone stopped to look in the direction I was pointing, then we all ran towards Dad to greet him. Somebody ran to tell Mum and she soon joined us.

Thrilled to bits, we all threw our arms around him, hugging and kissing him so much we almost toppled him over. We were so overjoyed we did not care that his unshaven face was so prickly. We skipped and danced around him joyfully, giggling uncontrollably as we went inside.

'Children, let Dad sit down, he is tired,' said Mum. We could already see the big load that had lifted off Mum's shoulders with Dad's safe return. This feeling of tremendous relief at having him back with us is etched in my memory to this day.

After Dad had dinner and a bath, the doctor was called to

check him over and his barber was called to give him a shave. The barber's shop was close by but closed by now, so he came to us. We younger kids went back outside to play some more, much happier now than before.

Dad finally recounted what had happened to him during the last week or so. He said it was powerful politicians and members of the communists who were responsible, that they had again been trying to persuade him to join the party, making big promises of a wealthy, prosperous life for him and his family. They became furious when he refused. He told how he had heard Mum knocking and pleading outside the office at the council chamber, but was forced to stay silent with a pistol held to his head. Then, in the darkness of the night with most of the town's people asleep and not a soul on the streets, he was blindfolded and taken to the railway station, and then by train to some unknown destination – which Mum had later learnt was the Futog police station. There they locked him in the basement in ankle-deep water, with a wooden structure resembling a bed but with no mattress or covering of any kind.

Over the next days the communists put more pressure on him to join them, but Dad held out.

'I will never become one of you. I will never do to others as you are doing to me,' he said.

'Then you will never see your family again,' his captor had said, putting a gun to his head.

Dad told how they then started to physically assault him, slapping his face and punching him in the stomach until he couldn't stand on his feet any longer.

But he continued to resist. 'I will never join you, for I could never treat people the way you are treating me.'

Dad said that he had been very afraid that he might not see us again, and that he had no idea what would happen to him next. But no matter what, he would not come down to their level.

This torture went on for days. Finally they realised that violence would not persuade Dad to join them. Before they set him free, he was told that he must not speak a word to anybody about what had been done to him in the lock-up or he could expect more of the same treatment. As a result of this threat, there was nowhere Dad could go to complain about the injustice done to him. The people in power were all in on it, united in their crime.

Once again we and the bakery returned to our normal routines, the customers knowing only that Dad had been a way for a while, probably arranging firewood and other supplies, as he often did.

The local government changed their tactics after Dad was released from Futog. Instead of trying to force him into *zadruga* with violence, they started taxing him at a higher and higher rate. Then they officially prohibited the sale of bread for cash, but only at my father's bakery. The other two bakeries in town continued as normal. Obviously this made it nearly impossible for Dad to make enough money for our family, though still he found a way to survive. I explained earlier how

Dad would exchange flour for bread in the bakery, which helped out farmers who didn't have much cash. When cash sales were banned, Dad had no choice but to do more bartering, exchanging bread for eggs, milk, fruit and vegetables and so on.

Many people in the town saw what the lawless government was doing to my family and were willing to support us ... though not everyone. A lady came into the shop one day with a small bag of wholemeal flour and asked to exchange it for an equal weight of white bread. Dad apologised that he couldn't do this. Most of the bread that Dad baked was white bread, but he only exchanged white bread for white flour because white flour was more expensive, being more processed than wholemeal flour. In these days, wholemeal bread – or 'black bread' as it was called in Serbia – was seen as the poor man's bread, though in our family we preferred it because it tasted much better. Anyway, this lady insisted that she wanted white bread, and Dad insisted that he could not give her white bread. Mum joined in and they stuck to their guns. Eventually the lady turned to walk away, and as she did so she said to my parents, 'You will regret this'.

'Oh dear,' said Mum after she had left. 'Trouble's coming. I know that lady is the wife of an important politician.'

Not long afterwards, four government officials came into the shop unannounced and demanded to search the premises. They saw that there was a lot of flour, then checked my father's business books. Deciding that some of the flour hadn't been accounted for, they stacked a number of bags of flour on top of each other right in the middle of the shop. Then they placed string over and around the stack and sealed it with wax. Dad was told he was not allowed to touch or use the sealed flour. He was given no other explanation and no time frame for how long he couldn't use the flour. Because the stack was so visible to customers, everybody knew that this was another act of reprisal against Dad, though if the government thought it would give them more support it didn't work.

A while later again, we children were playing chasey and hide-and-seek outside the bakery when a couple of policemen came past. They started chatting to us, asking if Mum and Dad were home and whether we'd had any flour delivered lately. We understood enough by now not to give straight answers, but one of my brothers snuck off and told Mum that the police were outside. There hadn't been a flour delivery, but because of the bartering Dad always had more flour than was on his books, so while the police were still talking to us kids, my parents and the older siblings were hurriedly hiding 50-kilogram bags of flour anywhere they could go – under the beds, in cupboards, even under the doonas. By the time the police went inside, nothing looked out of order. They checked the books but didn't search the house. Then they left. We never knew if they were really there to check on the flour, but by now we couldn't trust that they weren't. By this time Mum was even nervous if a policeman came into the shop just to buy bread.

Time went by without any further trouble, until early one morning when four men dressed in suits marched into the shop, claiming that they were tax collectors and had come to collect unpaid taxes. The shop was full of customers and Mum was on her own because Dad was away. Mum pleaded with them that she and Dad were very willing to pay their taxes, but they couldn't at the moment because they weren't allowed to sell bread for cash. She showed them the books to prove how much they were earning and how much they were spending keeping the family going. The men ignored Mum's pleading, saying that if the taxes couldn't be paid they would just have to confiscate our possessions. Most of us kids were in the house, still getting ready for school, when we heard this commotion coming from the shop, with Mum's voice rising as she became more angry and agitated.

'You know very well that the amount of tax imposed on us is outrageous,' she said. 'How can we pay more tax than what we earned? We can't give you money we haven't got. What this government is doing to us is a crime! How are we going to survive? We have nine children to provide for.'

The men ignored all of this. They eventually barged through the shop into the house, then moved from room to room as if it was their own home. They asked Mum to open the cupboards, but she refused – luckily someone had told her that they had no right to go through the cupboards. Finding nothing of any value, they continued out into our backyard, where there was a beautifully decorated horse carriage stored in the back corner. Someone had owed Dad some money some time before and, being unable to pay him in cash, they had given him this carriage, which he hadn't yet got around to selling. In the meantime, it had become a bit of a playground for us kids. These so-called tax collectors decided that this was worth confiscating and they started to push it out of the backyard and through our big side gate. Being early spring, there were a lot of puddles on the ground from melted snow, which made their job difficult. It was also hard to manoeuvre this big carriage around a corner to get it out. My older siblings went out and tried to stop them, which led to a bit of a tussle and one of the men slipped and fell into a muddy puddle, much to the amusement of the other men and us younger kids, who were watching all this go on. In the end, though, they did succeed in stealing the carriage.

This was the first of a number of similar raids. Sometimes Mum and Dad would get warning beforehand, giving them the chance to hide some things. Two crystal cabinets were removed to my aunt's place in the middle of the night one time. Other times we were all caught by surprise. Dad used to keep bees as a hobby and once they took his honey spinner – a device for removing honey from the honeycomb. They took most of our bikes, though not mine, as I jumped on it and rode it away. Eventually there was nothing left to take but our large dining room table with a big, heavy, central base, along with the matching chairs. It was very difficult to remove the table, which is probably why they left it until there was nothing else, but they took it anyway, leaving us with a totally empty dining room. Dad tried to buy that one back at an auction but was beaten to it by someone else, so we lost that.

This was obviously a tough time for our family, and especially for our parents. We often felt powerless and sad. But our parents were always very strong and they protected us from the worst, while doing their best to explain why all this was going on in a way that we could understand. I don't know whether they were faking it, but on the outside they stayed happy, which was enough for us to stay happy too.

Eventually Dad decided that he had had enough of this and would go and see Marshal Tito personally, to tell him how unfairly he had been treated. He collected all the relevant documents – all of his business books showing how much he was earning and how much he was spending on the business and the family, and on taxes. He took all this plus birth certificates and anything else he thought relevant, packed his case and caught the train to the capital, Belgrade. There, he went to the government building and requested to speak to Marshal Tito. Unsurprisingly, he didn't get to speak to Tito himself, but a representative did see him.

After Dad explained to the official what was happening, the man said, 'That is not possible; this should not be happening in our country,' but Dad showed him the evidence with his paperwork.

'You can see for yourself my income and amount of tax that is imposed on me,' said Dad.

'Well, Mr Vasic, I am aghast at what I hear and see. This should not happen to anybody. It is unjust. It seems to me that the administrative officials in Bački Petrovac are acting according to their own governing power.'

Eventually the official assured Dad that changes would be made and that he would be taxed fairly from now on. My father returned home with a sense of achievement and hope for better days to come. After several months there was a reshuffle in the council offices and a totally new person from a large city was moved in to Bački Petrovac with his family and put in charge. I don't remember anything about this man, but I do remember his wife, who was the first woman I ever saw smoking.

Within a few days of his arrival, this new councillor requested to be introduced to my father. Dad would tell us that the new politician was pleasant and had assured him that things would be better from here on.

'After all, Mr Vasic, you are a Serbian, like myself,' the councillor said. 'We have to take care of our own.'

And things did get better. The tax that Dad was asked to pay was lowered and the intimidation stopped.

But it didn't last. The new councillor didn't take long to be corrupted and the troubles for our family returned. Again lots of promise were made, but few were kept.

Amongst all these troubles, my family had another significant challenge to contend with.

In 1950, when my eldest brother Miro turned eighteen, he was conscripted to national service, something all Yugoslav males were obliged to do sometime between the ages of eighteen and twenty. Before this Miro had been working for a number of years with my father in the bakery; by now he was a qualified baker in his own right.

Miro in his national service uniform

After receiving his papers, Miro had no option but to travel to Novi Sad and join other young men at the Yugoslav Army base there. However, when it came to taking up a gun in the defence of his country, my brother could not make the required promise. Having fully adopted the Nazarene religion of our parents, Miro was a pacifist. He believed completely and literally in the commandment 'Thou shalt not kill'. The consequence of this was, as both he and my parents had expected, that he was taken straight to prison for refusing his national service, where he would serve a term of three years.

Over this time Miro was moved around a few times and Mum was constantly having to find out where he was so that someone could visit him. I remember going with Mum once. I think he was in a place called Kragujevac. We had to stand with a rope hanging across in front of us, and about a metre away was another rope that Miro had to stand behind. The gap between us was far enough that we could not reach out and touch each other. Other prisoners were separated from their visitors in the same way. A prison officer walked up and down this gap between prisoners and visitors, listening to what was being said. We were forced to speak Serbian rather than Slovak so that he could understand.

After Miro's eventual release, only a few months went by before he was drafted into the army again, and once more he refused to take up arms. This time he was sent to a much worse prison known as Goli otok. Goli otok is an island about three kilometres off the coast of northern Croatia. It is an extremely barren place – in fact its name means 'naked island' – which was made into a prison and labour camp for political prisoners in 1949. It was truly devoid of any vegetation, and of course was virtually impossible to escape from. The island was also very difficult to visit and visits were rarely permitted anyway.

Before Miro was imprisoned, he and Mum and Dad had planned a secret way of communicating in letters, knowing that all the prisoners' correspondence would be censored and that Miro would not be allowed to write in Slovak either. So when a letter arrived from Miro with only half of the page written on, the lower half of the page left blank, my parents knew it was a secret message. Mum carefully moistened the paper with cold water, then held the letter up to the light. Now it was possible to see, very faintly, a pressure imprint on the paper. The way this was done was that Miro had to wet the paper he was writing on, then place that paper on a very flat surface. He put another, dry, sheet of paper over the top and 'wrote' on that paper with a lot of force, making an impression on the wet page underneath. When that sheet had dried, there was no evidence of the impression he had made until my mother moistened it after it arrived. It must have been very difficult for Miro to do this in the prison without being seen, and perhaps he was only able to because he received the help of other inmates, probably those who were also conscientious objectors.

Unfortunately the news that Miro wrote to my parents this time was not good. He said that he was being tortured and was in fear of his safety. He asked that Mum and Dad come and see him as soon as possible. Of course my parents were terribly upset by this news. Without hesitation they organised for someone to take care of the bakery and shop and for my older sisters to take care of us younger ones. Mum made some cakes and biscuits for Miro and they left straight away, without any knowledge of when they would be back. I know they had a feeling of dread as they wondered what condition they would find Miro in.

Getting to Goli otok required a number of train trips and then finally a boat trip across to the island. When they finally got to see Miro, it was under strict supervision. As with other visits, they were not allowed to hug or touch each other in any way and nor were they allowed to speak Slovak. A prison guard watched and listened in to their conversation all the time. When the guard was looking the other way Miro was able to show Mum and Dad his injuries and sneak in a few Slovak words until the guard shouted, 'Speak Serbian'. Miro's arms were badly bruised and his hands were swollen and had some lacerations. When the guard turned his back again, Miro was able to pull down his collar and expose his injured neck, which had been chafed by a rope placed around it with heavy weights at each end. Miro had been forced to walk around in a circle with this weight around his neck until he fainted, then cold water was thrown over him. When he regained consciousness he was forced to carry the weights again until he fainted. This cycle was repeated over and over.

My parents left Goli otok with grief and heartbreak, unable to rescue their son from this dangerous and oppressive place.

Before they returned home, they stopped in Belgrade to complain to the relevant authority about Miro's maltreatment in prison.

'Who told you that?' asked the government official when he was told of Miro's injuries. 'Such things do not happen in our prisons.'

My parents had to be very careful in the way they responded to this. Miro would be in even more trouble if it was revealed that he had told them himself.

'No one told us,' said Dad. 'We saw his injuries ourselves when we were visiting him, just two days ago.'

'Who is inflicting these injuries on your son?'

Again my parents had to be careful. 'We assume other prisoners,' said Mum. This was the truth, but mainly because Miro's fellow inmates were promised privileges or given special benefits by the guards in exchange for their bad deeds. This kept the guards themselves out of trouble.

Miro

Of course my family were not the only ones finding life difficult under the Tito regime. In the period after World War II, the borders had been closed to emigration to prevent a flood of people leaving the country. Life had become too difficult for so many people, whether they were being pressured to join the communists (like my father), had had their business or farm forced into *zadruga* and could no longer make a living, or were being persecuted simply for voicing their opposition to the government. As our family experienced, the harassment never stopped. The only positive was that, when given a chance, the people would silently demonstrate their opposition to what was going on. One day the local authorities used the Bački Petrovac public announcement system (via loudspeakers all around the town) to decree that no one should buy bread from my father's bakery. The effect was the opposite of what they intended: a queue that stretched down the street further than ever before, and all the bread sold by nine o'clock in the morning.

Over time our family started to hear about people trying to leave. Some made their way to Ljubljana or Maribor, cities in Slovenia near the border with Austria. Others made their way to the border near the city of Trieste, an Italian city that until 1954 was controlled by British and American forces. These people then tried to reach the nearest border by walking through the forests, always moving very carefully so they weren't discovered by the dogs that were used to sniff people out. Many succeeded and were accepted as refugees by Austria or Italy. Others didn't make it, being caught and imprisoned or even killed.

Finally all the troubles and hassles and constant threat of imprisonment caught up with Mum and Dad. It was about five years since that first raid on our house in the middle of the night.

'Daniel, they are not going to leave us alone – there is always going to be something that they will find to cause us trouble. This harassment is not going to stop,' said Mum. 'What kind of future is there for us here? We have to get out of here somehow.'

Mum started singing a song she had made up: 'Daniel, we must get out of here; Daniel, we must get out of here'. She suggested that if we couldn't leave the country, maybe we could just move to another town, somewhere where nobody knew us. Dad never said anything, at least not that I heard.

Concerned about the risk of crossing out of Yugoslavia illegally, Mum decided to try and take a legal approach. She wrote a letter to some friends who were now living in Canada, asking if they would be kind enough to send us a guarantee and help us to get out of Yugoslavia. Several weeks later, the much-anticipated response arrived. Our friends were happy to help, and they could confirm that Canada would grant us entry visas and permanent residency as long as our friends were willing to guarantee that we would not be a burden on the Canadian government.

All that was now needed was for Yugoslavia to give us exit visas. This was very exciting news. Our whole family was filled with joy and cheerfulness and hope.

And then the Yugoslav government refused our application to leave.

Mum tried again, this time receiving a guarantee from the Nazarene church and some friends in Austria, but again our family's request to emigrate was rejected.

Mum kept singing, 'Daniel, we must get out of here; Daniel, we must get out of here'.

At one point – I didn't hear about this until much later – Dad met someone who offered to help smuggle our whole family across the border into Austria. He told Dad he had connections with the border guards in both Yugoslavia and Austria, and that if Dad gave him enough money he would be able to bribe these guards to let us through. Dad told this man that he was definitely interested, but asked him to check that the guards would let a large family of ten through, and to confirm how much it would cost.

Some weeks later the man met Dad again. He told Dad that the deal would only go ahead if the money was paid in advance. Dad agreed and gave the man the money he was asking for.

'I will get in touch with you to arrange a suitable date,' said the man.

And Dad never heard from him again.

The song continued. 'Daniel, we must get out of here.'

I was school age by now, about twelve years old, but I was still too young, at least in my parents' eyes, to be part of any of the discussions or decisions about when and how we might leave. After the government had refused our exit visas, things seemed to go quiet for a while, but even at my young age I couldn't help feeling that something was going on. Whenever I entered a room with Mum and Dad and my elder siblings in it, everybody suddenly stopped talking. All this whispering and mysterious behaviour made me wonder what was happening to my family. I hated this. It made me angry, troubled and concerned.

So what does a twelve-year-old do when her sense of security and safety is rocked? She resorts to eavesdropping. Catching a little piece of conversation here and another there, I started to put the puzzle together. As crazy as it sounded, it seemed like my parents were hatching a plan to get out of Yugoslavia illegally. What I couldn't work out was what that plan was.

Part Two

Escape

When Miro went off to military service and then to jail, that left Dad short of help in the bakery. Soon after, my sister Milinka, who was a teenager when Miro left, decided that she wanted to be a baker. She started helping Dad and doing an apprenticeship with him, which she eventually finished and became a qualified baker herself. The two middle boys, Daro (whose full name was Daroslav) and Vlado (Vladimir) also helped. Vlado was about seven or eight when Miro went away. They had responsibility for bringing firewood into the bakery and weighing it so Dad could get the oven to the correct temperature. They had to make sure that the copper had hot water in it too.

My two older sisters were more interested in dressmaking than in the bakery, and both started doing dressmaking apprenticeships. Veronka, the eldest, went away to the nearby town of Šid, while Ruženka was able to stay in Bački Petrovac. After a while Veronka came home – it didn't work out where she was. The place where she was working had a concrete floor on which the girls had to walk barefoot, which eventually gave Veronka bad pain in her hips. She had to receive injections for rheumatism when she got home. It turned out that she was really being used as a housekeeper while not learning very much about sewing at all, which made Mum angry, as Dad was paying for her apprenticeship.

When he was old enough, Daro also started an apprenticeship, though his was in shopkeeping. He worked for a Bata shoe shop – the same as Bata in Australia. Daro did very well. He was always a bit of comedian, so mothers with small children loved bringing them to see Daro. He invented all sorts of tricks to get reluctant children to try on their shoes. He was well liked by his manager, who had joined the communist party.

Amongst all this, with all of us living at home except poor Miro, I continued to feel like some sort of plotting was going on. I became jealous as well as annoyed about being kept in the dark when I found out that Vlado, only two years older than me, knew what was going on. However, that did mean that I could learn something from him, and on those occasions when the boys would let us 'babba' play soccer with them, I could learn something from the conversation. What I was able to gather was that there was a plan for all of us to get out of the country, and there was something about going on a goods train. Mum had bought a bag of mint lollies, which was very unusual as they were expensive, and I learnt that they would be used if one of us got a tickle in the throat on the train – sucking on a lolly would hopefully prevent us from coughing.

Nothing happened for a while. In the spring of 1956 my three eldest sisters – now nineteen, twenty-one and twenty-three years old – went away to help my Aunt Palenkaš on her farm. She was a widow, though she also had a brother who would help out. The farm was some distance away and because there was a *salaš*, or summer house, it was decided that the girls would stay there during the week and come home on weekends. This happened for a few weeks in a row, so after a while it just became normal for the girls to be away from home.

Then, all of a sudden, Mum became quite nervous. She seemed to always be in a hurry to greet the postman.

It would be some days before we understood the reason for Mum's anxiety – and why there was no way she could tell us what was going on. It would be some years before my siblings and I all learnt the detail of the story I can tell you now.

One of the long-running trades of Bački Petrovac is the manufacture of millet brooms. In the 1950s broom making was a big industry, with the local factory employing many local people. Brooms were exported on trains to destinations all over Europe. In each country a train passed through, it would stop in a major city and the carriage designated for that country would be removed before the train continued on its way.

My parents learnt that after these brooms left Bački Petrovac, they travelled through non-communist Austria on their way to the Eastern Bloc countries. Dad realised that if it could be worked out which carriage would be removed in Austria, perhaps we could stowaway on that carriage, hiding amongst the brooms. Of course we would need to be sure which carriage was to be removed in Austria, and we would need to take enough food and water with us to last a few days. It was risky, because if a mistake was made and we ended up on the wrong carriage, we could end up in another communist country and be in a lot of trouble, including being sent to jail. As it happened, we were related to one of the stationmasters at the Bački Petrovac railway station. Uncle John was a distant uncle, but still a relative. He would know exactly which carriage was destined for Austria, and he could help hide us in that carriage.

Dad decided to talk to Uncle John about this idea ... and that was about the end of it. Uncle John thought Dad was crazy. He pointed out that it was far too dangerous. He told Dad that sometimes the carriages were removed in a holding yard, sitting unopened for days at a time. There was no way to know how long it would take for a carriage to cross the border. And as they were sealed from the outside it would be impossible for anyone to get out. He also told Dad that there were too many of us. 'It would only take one child to sneeze or cough at the wrong time and you would be found out and thrown in jail,' he said. He also said that he would get sacked. 'I would never be able to get another job. I would be finished. I would probably be sent to jail too.' He told Dad to go away, that he didn't want to know about his plan.

But Dad didn't give up. He could not see another way out of Yugoslavia. He persisted with asking Uncle John for his help.

'John, you have to help us, we have to get out of this country,' Dad said. He kept explaining the troubles that he was dealing with: the constant pressure to join the communist party; the fact that there was no future for us in Yugoslavia.

John kept sending him away, but Dad kept returning, over and over again. He was like an annoying and irritating fly that keeps landing on your face no matter how many times you shoo it away. Dad kept offering more money as well, hoping that this would change our uncle's mind, but Uncle John was as obstinate as Dad was persistent.

Finally, at long last, Uncle John gave in, but on the condition that only a small group of the family would go. That would reduce the risks. At the time my younger siblings and I knew none of this – Mum and Dad felt it was too risky for us to know anything in case we spilled the beans – but my parents discussed the options with the older children. It was decided that Mum and Dad couldn't go first as they needed to stay and care for the rest of us, plus their disappearance would have raised suspicions. In the end my three eldest sisters put up their hands to go first.

Now there were more questions in my parents' minds. What would happen to the rest of us when Yugoslav authorities discovered that three members of the family had defected to Austria? Would Mum and Dad be in trouble? Would they be called to answer questions, or even jailed? Would Austria give the sisters refugee status, or would they deport them back to Yugoslavia?

In the end it was decided that the risk had to be taken. There was no other way. The girls would be hidden in a train carriage full of brooms destined for Austria, where they would ask for asylum.

This was when the girls were sent away to stay with Aunt

Veronka, Milinka and Ruženka

Palenkaš on her farm. It wasn't so they could work there – it was in order to reduce suspicion around town. In a town as small as Bački Petrovac, if the three girls had just disappeared with no reason, lots of people would have grown suspicious. It was possible that the alarm could have been raised before their train had got out of Yugoslavia and they would have been found and arrested. And sure enough, when the girls started going to the farm during the week, there were plenty of nosy locals who were asking Mum where they had gone. But, as I said earlier, after a few weeks everyone got used to the sisters being away. That part of the plan worked. Even my younger siblings and I became used to the older girls not being around. The time was finally right for the girls to attempt their escape.

The date for the sisters to attempt to stowaway was set as May 25, 1956.

At two o'clock in the morning on the chosen day – while the rest of us were fast asleep and none the wiser – the girls were taken to Bački Petrovac railway station in the horse-drawn carriage of my uncle and aunt Ruman. The time was chosen to minimise the chance that anyone would notice them. In the half-light, behind the station, well away from the public platform, they were met by Uncle John, who guided them to an isolated train carriage already packed with bundles of brooms. The carriage was like a small shipping container, with a sliding door on one side in which there was a single, small window with a sliding cover. This was the only place where air could get inside.

My sisters had with them just one small suitcase each. They had to take plenty of food and water because there was no way of knowing how long they might be in the carriage. They took enough food – including ham, salami and bread – to last them for fourteen days. Bundles of old newspapers were part of their supplies for when nature called – which hopefully wouldn't be too often as they wouldn't be eating much. This waste would be thrown out the window as the train was moving through the countryside at night. They also packed a few clothes, some books to keep them occupied and some blankets because, although it was May and heading towards summer, the nights were still quite cool.

Uncle John left the girls at the carriage to get themselves organised. By shuffling the brooms around, they were able to work their way into the middle of the carriage, shaping a cavity in the centre that they could sit in. Once they were in place the brooms were shuffled around again so that anyone outside – even if they opened the door – would have no idea that there was anything other than millet brooms filling the railway car, while not packing them so tightly that air wasn't able to get from the window to my sisters. It was hoped, too, that the smell of the millet would be enough to hide the girls from any sniffer dogs that might be used, especially near the Austrian border.

A little later Uncle John returned. He wished the girls good luck and sealed the door from the outside, as he did with every other goods carriage. After seeing the train off later that morning my uncle was able to let my parents know that the girls were on their way.

For Mum and Dad it was now a case of waiting for news. The rest of us thought our sisters were still at Aunt Palenkaš' farm.

With no easy access to the carriage's only window, it wasn't long before the girls had no idea where they were. Veronka, Ruženka and Milinka's train stopped at a number of different towns, but each time they had to stay deep inside the carriage, hidden by the brooms. They stayed very still and silent so that they would not be found. After a while they started to listen more carefully to what they could hear of any conversation outside. They weren't so much interested in what people were saying as they were in what language was being used. This was the only way they could work out where they were, which was very important, as it was critical that they didn't reveal themselves before they got into Austria. It was also critical that they *did* reveal themselves in Austria and got off the train before it travelled on to another Eastern Bloc country.

After five days they started to get very uncomfortable, squashed into their tiny moving home. Now the train stopped again. The girls wondered if they were finally in Austria, until they realised that most of the people outside were speaking Slovenian or Serbian. They made out the word 'Ljubljana' a number of times, so figured that's where they must be: in the capital of Slovenia. So they were close to Austria but not there yet. As cramped as they were, the girls had to stay hidden.

The train stayed at this station for hours, but finally started moving again. By now the three girls had really had enough. Ruženka, the second eldest, decided that they had to do something. They had to give themselves up at the next stop, whatever the consequences.

Some hours later their train ground to a halt again. This time they heard German language being spoken, though they still couldn't be sure they were actually inside Austria and not just at the border. If they were discovered at the border, there was a risk that Austrian guards would turn them over to the Yugoslav authorities on the other side. There had been stories of this happening, the Austrian guards being bribed to hand over refugees.

However, despite the risk, Veronka decided she had to find out where they were. She pushed enough brooms aside and carefully opened the window to have a quick look out. No sooner had she done so than a young man saw her. He called out, and Veronka panicked. *What have I done?* she thought. She shut the window and pushed back inside, petrified that she had given the game away by revealing herself too early. Then the carriage started moving forward, but it stopped after a short distance and then moved back some way.

The girls could now hear a young man calling out, 'Zuska, where are you?' He was moving up and down the train, calling out and knocking on the doors. It seemed that because the train had moved he no longer knew in which carriage he had seen the girl at the window. But he also must have recognised that Veronka was Slovak, and not Austrian, presumably because of her plaits. He was using a common Slovak name, Zuska, and was calling out in the Slovak language. However, his accent was thick – he clearly wasn't using his own language.

What should they do? Should they take a risk with this young man?

Finally they decided that they had no option. They could stay squashed into this carriage no longer. Now they all made their way to the window and revealed themselves. Soon afterwards some police arrived with cutters to remove the lock on the door and the girls were helped down from their broom-filled room, thankful more than anything to finally stretch their legs. After nearly a week squashed into this space, they were very wobbly on their feet and found themselves needing help to walk.

To their great relief, my sisters were not arrested but instead were welcomed by the local people of Kufstein, in Austria, where the train had stopped. It turned out that three young women arriving as stowaways was a very unusual thing in a small town like Kufstein. By the time they were released from the train carriage, the media had also arrived. The girls were blinded by flashes from the news reporter's camera, and their story was later told in the local newspaper.

They were taken to the police station and had their identity papers checked. The next day they were interviewed by Interpol to have their story verified and to ensure that they weren't running away from some crime. Once they were given the all clear, they were told they could stay in Austria as refugees, or they could apply to move to any other country that was accepting refugees. They decided that they would like to go to Australia – we already knew a family, the Makovnik family, who had moved from Bački Petrovac to Melbourne a few years earlier – so they made an application. They had heard all sorts of stories about Australia: that everyone had gold in their backyard if they just dug down to about a metre; that they needed single girls so any single woman who emigrated there would be given a car. A couple of days after they arrived in Austria they were placed with local farmers to work as farm hands while they waited for permission to emigrate to Australia.

Mum finally received a letter from our sisters a few days after they had arrived in Austria. It was the first time she knew that their journey had been a success, and she was enormously relieved. Finally she was able to tell us that the girls weren't at Aunt Palenkaš' farm anymore ... they were in Austria! She wouldn't tell us how they got there – that was to remain a secret (though from my eavesdropping I knew it had something to do with trains and brooms). Of course many of the details remained unknown to her as well, and would be until we were finally reunited with the girls much later.

One exciting thing that happened after the girls arrived in Austria was that they sent us a parcel. It included chewing gum, which we had never seen before, and also a plastic can, like a small plastic bucket holding about two litres. This became an object of a lot of fascination because plastic was a very new thing. I would carry it to the farmer who we bought milk from and along the way people in the street would stop me to ask what this thing was. Once even a horse-drawn carriage pulled up beside me because its driver wanted to have a look.

Six months after they arrived in Austria, the girls were granted entry to Australia. They didn't go by boat but instead by air, which was very rare in those days. It was something to do with the Suez Crisis that had caused the Suez Canal to be closed. I remember bragging about this at school – that my sisters were flying all the way to Australia. They arrived in Melbourne on December 13, 1956. It was not long after the Melbourne Olympic Games, so Melbourne was quite famous around the world at the time. The Makovnik family met them at the airport and not long afterwards they were sent to a hostel in the western suburbs of the city. There they lived in Nissen huts – half-cylindrical buildings covered in corrugated iron – which were very widely used in migrant hostels in Australia for many years. The first thing we heard from them was that they did not like the climate: it was summer in Melbourne, which can be very hot. They also reported that they didn't like the water, that the fruits were all different – and of course there were no free cars and no one was finding gold in their backyard. And with almost no English, they found it very hard to find work.

Not long after they arrived in Australia, my second sister, Ruženka, married a man called Alfonz – a Czechoslovak man who had been introduced to her by the Makovniks. Mum wasn't at all happy about this. She had agreed with the sisters that none of them would marry until we were all out of Yugoslavia. The other girls then moved to Adelaide, because there were some Nazarene people in that city. They continued to write to us, saying that Australia wasn't what they expected, and that if they didn't have to stay for two years minimum – a condition of their government-paid passage to the country – they would have moved to Canada.

One of my cousins was about three months older than me and also called Anna. There were a lot of Annas in Bački Petrovac. Her family had a house cow that Anna would take out into a farmer's paddock to graze during the summer when there was no school. Farming land was not fenced in at that time, so Anna's job was to make sure the cow didn't stray too far. Sometimes she asked me to go with her, which I loved to do. We would pick wild blackberries, or sneak into someone's vineyard and help ourselves to a few grapes, or make mud pies and throw them at each other. Mum didn't like this last game very much!

Not long after we had heard from my sisters, I was with Anna and her cow. I knew I wasn't supposed to share our news, but I was just busting to tell someone. And if I couldn't tell my cousin, who could I tell? I made her promise to keep it a secret, which of course she did. Who doesn't want to hear a secret? I then spilled the beans. I told Anna everything I knew: about the girls having escaped to Austria and it having something to do with a train full of brooms. I probably embellished a fact or two where I didn't really know the truth.

Later, when I was coming home from a friend's house, I found Mum and Dad waiting for me out the front with my Uncle Paul, Anna's father. Well, did I cop it! It turned out that Anna had gone home and straight away told her father everything that I had told her. Now Mum was in a panic.

'How did you know all that?' asked Mum. 'Do you know we could go to prison if this news gets out? And so could your Uncle John. Or he could lose his job. Do you realise how hard this might make it for us?'

Dad wasn't in quite such a panic as Mum – perhaps with his tendency to trust people, he understood why I had done what I had done. But he was angry with me. I was sent to my room, grounded and not allowed to play with anyone for a few days.

I felt very stupid, and I had also learnt a harsh lesson about expecting others to keep secrets. I don't think I've forgiven Anna even now, so many years later.

About six months after the older girls' success it was decided that my father and my two older brothers, Daro and Vlado, would follow in the same way (with Miro still in prison). Of course I wasn't told anything – they weren't going to trust me with any secrets now. All I knew was that after one Saturday night it was very quiet around the house, with only my mother at home with her three youngest children: myself, Elenka and Branko.

That evening, Daro's manager from the Bata shoe shop knocked on the door. He wanted to know where Daro was. He was very insistent, even getting a bit aggressive, asking over and over where Daro was. Of course Mum couldn't tell him, so she just avoided the question. He eventually went away, though he returned the following morning. He still didn't get an answer to his question. That morning, when Mum came back from church, some friends came to tell her that they had been past the shoe shop and noticed the manager was inside doing stocktaking. They thought this was unusual, as he had done the same thing not long ago. Later that evening we heard that the manager had been in the pub. He had got quite drunk and was loudly saying that Daro had stolen 10,000 dinar, which was a lot of money. When Mum heard about this she knew it wasn't true, but she was worried. It was clear that the manager knew that Daro had gone away, though exactly how much he knew Mum wasn't sure.

A couple of days later I received some strange news from a teacher at my school, of all people.

'I saw your two brothers on a bus in Novi Sad. They were being escorted by the police.'

My mother was very worried when I told her this. By now the boys and Dad should have been just about in Austria. Something must have gone wrong.

For a few days we heard nothing at all, and then Daro and Vlado arrived home unannounced. They told us how they had got as far as Ljubljana, the last stop before the train would have crossed into Austria. However, this time sniffer dogs were used to check every single carriage and the police easily found Dad and the boys. Daro said it was like the police knew exactly where to look, which only reinforced the idea that they had been reported by someone. They said that Dad had been arrested and was in jail in Belgrade for four months, but the boys had been released because they were under age.

Obviously this was very bad news about Dad, but Mum was pleased to have the boys home safely.

When Mum told Daro about his boss and the accusations he made, Daro's eyes narrowed.

'I trusted him,' he said. 'I thought he was my friend.'

Daro decided that he should turn himself into the police, given the accusations his manager had made about him, but the police told him just to go home.

Several weeks later, the manager came to our home and

greeted Daro in a friendly manner as if nothing had happened, but of course Daro was not so pleased to see him.

They had a heated discussion (which I happened to overhear – I still had the art of eavesdropping). At one point Daro said, 'Hey Boss! Now I know why you were altering those figures in the financial account books. It was you who was trying to swindle Bata Shoes. Then you tried to pin it on me.' They parted ways on angry terms.

The next weekend Daro went to the pictures with his friends. As Mum was getting ready for bed about ten o'clock, there was a sudden and very loud thump on her bedroom window, followed by the sound of someone running and a voice calling out. It was hard to tell, but Mum said later that she thought the voice was familiar. She opened the front door and could see two figures fighting in the dark, shadowed from the street lamps by a large tree in front of the house next door. She soon realised that one of the figures was Daro, so she shouted out loudly: 'Somebody help! Someone is bashing up my son!'

Very soon we all joined Mum outside to see what was going on. Some neighbours came out of their house across the road and shone a torch onto the two people wrestling with each other and immediately one of the men withdrew. He pulled his collar up high, apparently in an attempt to hide his face, then briskly walked away.

Daro told us he had been ambushed in front of our house. He had managed to get away briefly, which is when he knocked on Mum's window. He said that he knew for sure that it was his manager, even though the attacker had tried to stay in the dark. The neighbour's torch had revealed all.

Daro was not hurt, but he was badly shaken and we were all distressed, especially Mum. My brother did not want to involve police, as he didn't trust them anymore, so basically the whole incident was forgotten. People in our neighbourhood knew it was better to keep your head down and not ask any questions rather than risk getting involved.

Some time later there was a court case when Daro sued his boss for defamation of character. The result of this was that Daro's name was cleared, as his boss could not support the public accusations he had made. Daro was keen to have an announcement clearing his name published in the newspaper but was told that that would not be appropriate, given the accusations against him were never published in the first place. The manager was required to pay the court's costs, but at Mum's request he did not receive any further fine. Mum knew that the manager's wife was pregnant and she didn't want to see the wife penalised for her husband's actions.

Three months later Dad finally arrived back home. He had been in this large Belgrade prison for three months, not four, having been released early on good behaviour. I remember going to see him once with Mum during this time. We took some camomile tea in that plastic container that the girls sent, and this time it was a source of fascination for the prison guards.

'Have a look at this. It isn't breakable,' they were saying. 'It's safe. No one could do any damage with it.'

Now that Dad was with us again, we were back where we started, with only the three girls safely out of Yugoslavia.

Sometime around the end of 1956 another of our uncles – another Uncle John – came to visit. He lived in Czechoslovakia and was taking advantage of some newly relaxed travel arrangements. Previously, people living in the Eastern Bloc countries weren't allowed to leave their home country, just like us in Yugoslavia. Now, it was possible to travel between the Eastern Bloc countries. This arrangement included Yugoslavia, even though it was an independent communist country, not controlled by the Soviet Union. All of a sudden many people started visiting relatives in Czechoslovakia, Hungary, Romania and so on.

Fairly soon after this, rumours started to circulate about some people taking advantage of this situation. An acquaintance of my parents went to Czechoslovakia as a tourist, but never came back. It turned out that to get to the Slovakian city of Bratislava you had to travel by train to Vienna and change trains there for the final leg. When this person's train stopped in Vienna, he turned himself in to the Austrian police and asked for asylum, which was granted.

'Well if he can do that so can we,' said my mother. 'I will write to John and have him send us the guarantee.' This was a guarantee that he would look after us and that we would not be a burden on the local government, and it was a necessary part of the application for an entry visa. 'This will be our ticket out of Yugoslavia.'

Dad agreed that it was worth a try.

By now Daro was a bit older – almost eighteen. He was now working with a theatre company as an actor and comedian, which he was happy to keep doing. He didn't want to let the company down. Mum and Dad weren't too pleased about this, but he was clear about his decision. My parents applied for themselves plus their four youngest children – Vlado, myself, Elenka and Branko – to travel to Czechoslovakia (now Slovakia).

Eventually the required paperwork arrived from the Czech government, although that wasn't the end of it. My parents now had to apply for permission to leave Yugoslavia, and this is where things got a bit more complicated. Immediately my father's application was rejected. He'd just been released from jail for trying to escape the country illegally – they weren't about to let him go legally.

Again Mum and Dad started talking in hushed tones, forcing me to eavesdrop.

'You must go without me,', Dad told Mum. 'Take the children and go.'

'But I can't leave without you. What if they reject me in Austria as a single mother with four children?'

'I don't think they will do that,' said Dad. 'And I think once you're there the authorities here will let me go on humanitarian grounds.'

In the end I think the draw to leave was too great. Mum didn't give me any details, but I could tell from watching her that she was making preparations for us to leave.

One of the things Mum had to do before we left was let Miro know what we were planning, but of course she had to do this very secretly. If the prison guards found out about our plan, Mum would probably be arrested herself. The way she did get the message to Miro was very clever. It was normal for prisoners to receive parcels from their families, often containing food that they could share with each other. However, this food would be checked by the guards to make sure that it didn't contain any weapons or other contraband. The guards would usually slice a cake or strudel right down the middle from end to end, and then again across the cake's width. Now, as Mum knew this was what they were doing, she would write a note onto a tiny piece of paper and roll it up very small. She would then roll it into the unbaked pastry of a poppy seed or walnut strudel, right in the corner at the point where she sealed the pastry. In this way the note would not be revealed by the guard's cuts. Miro knew this, so when he received a strudel from Mum, he made sure that he kept the end pieces for himself. So in this way Mum was able to let Miro know our plans.

A day came when Mum told us we should pack our suitcases. Perhaps learning from the dangers of keeping things secret from us, only to have me blurt them out, this time she revealed the plan, though only on the day before we were to leave.

'Tomorrow we will be getting on a train to Czechoslovakia, but when we change trains in Vienna, in Austria, we will ask for asylum in that country. It is very important that you do not tell anyone about this. I don't know how it is going to work out and they may even send us home again and I might have to go to prison. We have to keep it very secret. You cannot tell anyone, and you cannot say goodbye to any of your friends.'

This last part was the hardest. On the last day of September in 1957, my friend Mary called for me on the way to school, as she did every day. After school she came home so we could do our homework together. I knew that I would not be at school the next day, but I had to pretend that everything was normal. When she went home that night I was very sad at the idea that Mary would call the next morning and I wouldn't be there. Later that afternoon I met my cousin Anna in the street. I so much wanted to give her a big hug and say goodbye, but with Anna I knew that that would be a very bad idea. This time I managed to keep my secrets to myself.

It seemed darker than normal at about four o'clock in the morning of October 1, 1957. But then I didn't really know how dark it usually was at that hour, as I was normally fast asleep.

Our uncle and aunt Ruman were waiting for us with their horse-drawn carriage at the end of the street – they didn't want to come down the street in case it woke the neighbours. Quickly and quietly we shuffled down the street with our bags, and everything was loaded onto the carriage. The cart had a canvas cover that hid us from the world, just in case anyone was awake at this hour. We all snuggled together in silence as we rattled down the gravel road to the station. I was excited by the adventure, but also anxious. Would I ever see my home again?

We were met at the station by another aunt, Mum's sister, and a friend of hers. Both were members of the Nazarene congregation. With our bags off the carriage, we huddled together in the cold and waited for the train. It seemed to take a long time, but perhaps we were just impatient. Then, finally, the train was visible. Dad gave us all big hugs, and I'm sure Mum was crying in his arms. We had no idea when we would see him again – or even if we would.

There was no platform at the Bački Petrovac station, so Dad had to help lift us and our bags up into the train. It was quite a small train – this was just a local service that would take us to Belgrade. Once we were all set, Dad slammed the heavy carriage door shut behind us.

I can't imagine how Mum felt at that moment.

At first we sat in silence. I guess everybody was feeling sad, as I was, leaving Dad behind, thinking how lonely it would be for him to return to an almost empty house. Our big house that used to vibrate with eleven people's lives would now have just Dad and Daro living in it, and Dad would be running the bakery and the shop with only one assistant. All he had to look forward to was, hopefully, a letter from Austria.

As we and the other passengers started to wake up a bit more, I began to feel more excited about what was ahead of us. I had enough Serbian language to chat to some of the passengers and I remember at one point Mum told me to stop being so giggly – I was drawing too much attention to myself.

Before too long we arrived at the main railway station in Belgrade, where we all disembarked. We found our way to the right platform for our next train – the one that would take us all the way to Vienna – and then we waited. It seemed like we waited forever, but 'forever' isn't really that long when you're twelve years old. It may only have been a couple of hours, though it could have been longer. People hustled and bustled along the platform while porters pushed luggage trolleys up and down. A couple of us jumped on an empty one of these to have a bit of a ride. For kids from a small town this was all very exciting.

Finally we boarded the train bound for Vienna and now settled in for a long, overnight trip. So far so good, though of course we were still in our own country.

'Tickets, please. Tickets, please.'

The conductor's voice jolted everyone from their sleep. It was still dark outside, though I have no idea what time it was. After our tickets were checked a Yugoslav border security guard came along, checking everyone's passports and other papers before the train crossed into Austria. Looking across at Mum, even my twelve-year-old self could tell that she was very nervous, but the guard inspected our papers without a word and moved on.

The train rolled forward, but only a short distance. We were over the border and now the Austrian officials needed to check our papers. My main memory is of how strange their language was, and of Mum's other concern: the two feather doonas she had brought with her. She knew feathers were not supposed to be taken into Austria without fumigation, so she didn't want them to be detected. A friend of ours was particularly skilled at folding doonas up very tightly. He had managed to get these ones into quite a small parcel, so it didn't look anything like as big as normal. It worked. When the guard kicked the parcel and asked, 'Was ist das?' Mum told him it was just a bed cover. He didn't say anything else.

Now the train moved again and we all looked at Mum as she breathed out a big sigh of relief.

'We are on Austrian soil,' she said.

And with that we all went back to sleep.

It was mid-morning when the train pulled into the station at Vienna. As soon as it stopped, Mum told us to gather all our things together – we all had something to carry.

'Do you have your coat, Anna?' she asked.

I held up my heavy green winter coat to show her.

When she was happy that we weren't leaving anything behind, Mum ushered us all off the train and onto the busy platform. The station was enormous and there were so many people moving in every direction.

'Come on everyone,' urged Mum. On the train she had told us that the first thing we had to do was leave the station and get as far away as we could. But it wasn't easy. We were still small children and carrying our bags was tiring. Still, we didn't really need to worry about being discovered or standing out from the crowd – the crowd was just too big for anyone to stand out.

We walked down a number of streets, having no idea where we were going, until eventually the crowd had dwindled and we were more or less on our own. Finally we were allowed to put our bags down in a quiet place and have a rest.

'Stay here,' Mum said to us. 'I'm going to find a public telephone and call the man who can help us.'

So now we waited, four young children on a quiet Vienna street, surrounded by our belongings. We didn't say much to each other, rather just sitting there wide eyed and trying to come to terms with this new world.

After a little while a very well-dressed older man approached us, taking a bar of chocolate from his pocket and offering it. This time I was transported back to home and those visits to my aunty's house, where we had been taught to politely decline offers of biscuits and sweets. Unfortunately our 'No, thank you' didn't translate very well and the man seemed to take offence. He returned the chocolate to his pocket and walked away, mumbling something to himself. I didn't feel good about offending this man, so when a lady came out of her house across the road from where we were waiting and offered us some tea from a dainty pot she was carrying, we gratefully accepted, doing our best to say *danke schön*. She beckoned me to come with her to her doorway, where she gave me a few coins, all the time chattering away in Austrian and me not understanding a word. Again I tried to say thank you. To this day I still feel some guilt at offending the old man.

Finally Mum returned. 'Mr Kopčok is coming,' she said. 'He is someone from Bački Petrovac who now lives here in Vienna.'

Mr Kopčok arrived and soon after him a taxi pulled up. Mr Kopčok helped us load our luggage and then spoke to the driver, who took us to a large building that we quickly worked out was a police station. We carried all our bags inside and soon a policeman found someone who could speak Slovak. Mum explained that we were seeking asylum in Austria. After a few minutes Mum told us that she would need to be interviewed. We children were shown to a waiting room, where we sat for about an hour and a half, though it felt like much longer.

When Mum finally came to get us, she told us that we would be taken in a police van to somewhere to stay the night. We would then have to go to a detention centre for a while, maybe a few weeks, while our story was checked with Interpol, the international police network. 'But don't worry,' Mum said, 'we will all be kept together. Gather up your bags again. And don't forget your coat, Anna.'

By now we were all so tired that we didn't really care where we went, though I do remember Vlado was very excited about the idea of going for a ride in a police van, though I'm not sure why. It wasn't very comfortable, sitting in the back with wooden benches on either side.

It was getting dark by the time we stopped, and we were asked to get out of the van. I don't know where we were, but we were shown to a large room in which there were already probably forty people spread out in rows across the floor. We were given blankets to lie on and to cover ourselves with, then found a spare space on the floor and made ourselves as comfortable as we could. A couple in front of us, with two girls a bit younger than me, were arguing all the time, but other than that there wasn't a lot of talk in this hall, just the murmur of whispers. It was all very gloomy, but we were so exhausted by now that before long, despite the discomfort, we were all asleep.

The next day we were on the move again, this time in

another police van. They took us to a real prison, a section of which was operating as a detention centre for refugees.

After we arrived Mum told us she was going to be interviewed again. This time we children were taken to a room with the word *Spielzimmer* on the door, which I would later understand meant playroom. But this wasn't a playroom for children – it was the recreation room for the refugees, where they could play cards or chess and so on. We were given some sandwiches then left alone, the door locked behind us.

Once again we found ourselves waiting.

And waiting.

We could hear people moving around outside this room, but we couldn't see anything. There was a small peep hole in the door which someone seemed to open every now and again, presumably to check on us.

Having done so much waiting lately we were starting to get used to it, though after what seemed like three or four hours we did start to fret. Why were they keeping Mum for so long? What were they doing with her? There wasn't much we could do but keep waiting, but I know I was getting more and more worried and I could see that my sister and brothers they were obviously feeling the same. I think we were close to panic by the time the door finally opened and Mum reappeared, looking red in the face and very, very tired.

'Where were you for so long?' we all asked Mum, but she just took a deep breath and sighed. She'd had enough questions for one day. Later she would explain that she had had to explain why we were seeking asylum, including all the details of the way the communists had threatened our family. She had to show all her documents and they had to be checked for authenticity. And they had just asked so many questions, making sure Mum's story checked out from every direction.

We were now taken into the detention centre. There was a long hallway with cells on either side and wooden tables with bench seats along the centre. Vlado, even though he was only fourteen years old, was taken to the men's section. Mum was given a cell with two portable beds for Elenka and Branko, now ten and eight respectively, while I, as a twelve-year-old, was given a cell of my own across the hall from them. The cells were plain, but had comfortable beds and each had a toilet and hand basin. Thankfully all of this wasn't a complete shock, as Mum had heard from other families who had left Bački Petrovac before us, and she had explained what would probably happen. Nevertheless, we were very young to be in prison cells.

We must have been very hungry on that first night in the detention centre because to this day I can remember what we were given to eat. We were all called out of our cells and had to sit at one of the long tables. There we were given sausages with gravy and mashed potatoes. We met some of the other refugees, who were from all over Yugoslavia, plus some from Hungary, Romania, Bulgaria and other Eastern Bloc countries. Mostly we couldn't communicate with these people due to the language barrier, though we did meet a Slovak lady who Mum knew from a neighbouring town to Bački Petrovac.

During the day the cell doors were left open and we could move around, including visiting the men's area where our brother Vlado was staying. We were allowed outside too at times, though only into an exercise yard that had a small garden at its centre. As much as we could we would chat with other people, which is how we heard the horror stories of others' escapes from their countries. There was a couple who defected from Bulgaria in a large truck by crawling into toolboxes attached to the truck's chassis, one on each side. Each box was not much bigger than a suitcase. The Slovak lady had come by train as we had.

At night we were all locked in our cells. In the morning we were woken with keys rattling and guards calling, 'Get up, come on, get up!'

Other 'inmates' had told us to make sure that our beds were well made every morning as the guards would come around to inspect our cells after breakfast. As a result, on the first morning we returned to our cells to tidy up and straighten the beds. Mum made Elenka and Branko's beds then moved on to her own, while Branco sat on his bed eating a bread roll.

Sure enough, soon the guards were moving down the hallway from cell to cell. All was quiet until they arrived at Mum's cell. Then, all of a sudden, all hell broke loose. The guards were shouting at the top of their voices, waving their arms and pointing. The racket filled the hall, but Mum couldn't understand a word they were saying. Next thing one of the guards was in the cell, pulling all the sheets and blankets off Branko's bed.

I ran across to see Mum. 'What's wrong? What's happened?' I asked.

Soon a small crowd had gathered as the people from all the surrounding cells tried to see what was going on, while all the time the guards kept screaming what sounded like commands in German.

Mum was pale and trembling now. She would tell me later that she still had memories of the Germans occupying Yugoslavia in the war, and this brought those memories right back.

Finally someone arrived who could act as an interpreter. As she spoke to the guards the noise died down.

'This bed was not tidy,' she said, pointing to Branko's bed. 'Someone was sitting on it and there were breadcrumbs on the bed, and there are breadcrumbs on the floor too.'

'That is all?' Mum managed to ask.

'Yes, that is it.'

For all the noise and the pulled-apart bed you would think that the guards had come across a murder scene. They really were treating us just like prisoners.

It was our first morning in the prison and it upset Mum for the rest of the day, but of course Branko wasn't allowed to eat a roll in his cell anymore!

The next day some guards brought a portable bed into my cell. A girl a little older than me, probably about sixteen years old, was to share my cell. She was Hungarian and had escaped from her country with her father. It was very difficult for both of us because we could not communicate at all. We didn't even know each other's names. She spent most of her time with her father in the next corridor, where all the men stayed. Later

I would learn that this girl had lost her mother and that her father had experienced some kind of trauma.

A few days later I needed to use the toilet. Not wanting anyone to walk in on me and catch me on the 'throne', I asked Elenka and Branko to guard the door of my cell and not let anybody in until I was finished. Unfortunately my 'cell mate' returned at just this time. She wanted to come into the cell but my siblings blocked her way, trying to ask her to wait a few minutes. Of course she had no idea what they were saying and could not understand why these two wouldn't let her into her own cell. She started to cry and shrill and then ran screaming to find the guards. In no time four guards arrived to see what was happening, but they couldn't communicate with Elenka and Branko either. There was such a commotion, and in the meantime I'm just trying to do my business. It was so embarrassing – I can still feel the embarrassment today. Finally a lady who spoke both Hungarian and Yugoslav languages arrived and she was able to explain why my siblings were standing guard, but it was all a bit too late to avoid my embarrassment and this girl's frustration.

Soon after this the guards came back and removed the portable bed. The girl was moved somewhere else and I never saw her again.

Asten Lager

Just under three weeks after we arrived at the detention centre, on October 17, 1957, I celebrated my thirteenth birthday. Although 'celebrate' is the wrong word. The truth is that this birthday came and went with no one noticing, and I decided to keep it to myself. I knew Mum was still very worried about the uncertainty of whether or not we would be allowed to stay in Austria. She was also worried about whether Dad would be able to join us. She had plenty on her mind.

Ten days later Mum was summoned to the office. When she came back, she was walking much straighter and I'm sure there was almost a smile on her face. She held up a card as she came towards us – an identity card for Austria.

'We have been given permission to stay in Austria,' she told us, her face lighting up. 'We will be released from this place in the next few days and relocated to a refugee hostel. There we can wait and hopefully Dad will join us, and after that we can either stay in Austria or apply to move to another country.'

Sure enough, early in the morning a few days later we were told to pack up our bags. Once again Mum checked with me that I had my coat before we, along with a number of other refugees and a guide, were given some sandwiches and put on a train. We then travelled for a few hours west of Vienna. We arrived at a place called Asten, which was a very small town that seemed to be in the middle of nowhere. We walked with our bags to a place called Asten Lager – Asten Hostel – which we were told was an army barracks that had been converted to a camp for refugees.

By now we were getting used to moving around, and we were definitely excited that this place straightaway felt better than the prison we had been in.

We were shown to a barracks building – number 3. At the entrance was a small sheltered area before two large swinging doors that made a swooshing sound as they swung closed. On the left there was a laundry and on the right a shared bathroom, before you got to the wide hallway that stretched from one end of the building to the other. On either side of this corridor I counted fifteen rooms, making thirty in total. At the far end of the hall were two more swinging doors leading to the outside.

Our room was number 15, and it also had our family name on the door. It was much larger than the cells we had just left, with all five of us able to share the same room, so at least we could be together. There was a small table and chairs, two sets of bunk beds and a single bed, each bed having a heavy hessian mattress, pillows, sheets and three grey woollen army blankets that were so heavy we could hardly lift them, let alone sleep under them. There was soap, washing powder and towels, along with plates and cutlery. There was also a small wood stove on which it was possible to heat some water.

Mum was given thirty shillings as spending money, which

she would be given every week. It turned out this wasn't all the money we had. Finally Mum revealed why she had always been checking that I had my coat since we left Bački Petrovac. She had sewn quite a lot of money into the lining of the coat! This had been a bit risky, as we probably would have got into trouble if it had been discovered in Yugoslavia, but somehow we had made it this far without the secret being discovered or me losing my coat. I'm not sure I would have been so trusting that a twelve-year-old wouldn't lose a piece of clothing!

Once we had dumped all our stuff into our new room, it was time to find something to eat. We were tired and hungry after another long journey. Unfortunately access to food wasn't straightforward, and in fact was quite stressful. Mum found some neighbours who spoke Serbian and they explained that we had to walk to the communal kitchen for our meals, which was nearly a thirty-minute walk. The idea was to take large containers to the kitchen then bring the food back to the barracks. This created a problem, because we hadn't been provided with any containers. The neighbours kindly lent us theirs for the moment. They were made from empty food tins of about two litres capacity, with wire handles secured through holes pierced on opposite sides. At the kitchen we had to present a meal ticket and a hole was punched into this for each meal. Our first meal was something resembling Hungarian goulash with a crusty bread. After lunch these nice people showed us where we could find empty food tins – discards from the kitchen – and wire to make our own cans, so that became a job for Vlado and Branko. By dinner time we were organised.

Just after we finished our lunch on that first day, we had a nice surprise when we were visited by a man we knew well from Bački Petrovac. Mr Demrovski had arrived in Asten Lager six months before us.

Nourished and rested the next day, it was time to get our room into order.

There was a small wardrobe in the room, so we were able to hang some of our clothes in there. What didn't fit stayed in our suitcases, which we stored under the beds. We also had the doonas with us that Mum had smuggled out of Yugoslavia, and we decided that these should be for Mum herself, one underneath her to soften the bed and one on top. It was nearly November, so would soon be getting colder.

My memory of the first night in this place was just how quiet it was. You could hear any sound. If someone went to the toilet you would hear their footsteps on the wooden floorboards. If someone came or went from the building you would hear the swoosh of the doors as they closed, and it was easy to tell which doors – from which end of the building – were being used.

The next morning Elenka, Vlado and Branko went to collect breakfast from the kitchen, while Mum and I stayed to continue tidying our room. Finally, after breakfast there was time for us kids to explore our new surroundings. There were rows and rows of barracks like ours – there must have been at least forty buildings. There were some for families, some for single men and a Jewish section as well, which was a bit separate from the rest. From the language that we could hear, it seemed that most people were from Yugoslavia.

In the meantime, Mum went to the office to get some more information about the hostel. We had no idea how long we would be in this place – it could be years – so she needed to know what was what. She also had to find out how to send a letter back home so she could tell Dad where we were. She was told that she must carry her identification with her at all times. We were free to come and go from the hostel, and even to have visitors. Visitors had to be reported at the office if they intended to stay overnight. She learnt about the school, too, and enrolled Elenka, Branko and me into the primary school that had been established in the grounds of the hostel. Vlado was too old for primary school, so avoided going to school altogether, as there was no high school in the hostel.

Our first weekend arrived and we were surprised to be given extra food at lunchtime. As well as a hot meal, there were bread rolls and cold cuts like salami. Vlado ate all of his share quickly, before one of the neighbours pointed out that the cold food was for our dinner. On weekends the kitchen didn't serve food at night. We still had a lot to learn. Vlado, however, wasn't bothered.

'God will provide,' he said.

Sure enough, that afternoon a man came knocking on our door and he gave us 'milk cards'.

'With these cards you may go to the dairy and you are eligible to receive four litres of milk each day for free,' said the man.

'I told you God will provide,' said Vlado, laughing as he went off to get some milk.

Around that same time, we kids were roaming around and we spotted a Slovak lady in the next building. We could tell she was Slovak because of what she was wearing, which was a traditional headdress, embroidered blouse and an embroidered skirt. She wasn't from Bački Petrovac – her costume was not what women wore in our home town – but she was definitely Slovak. We ran screaming back to Mum to tell her. Mum would love to talk to someone in her native language. Mum went and found her and reported back to us that the lady had a husband and young child and that she had come from a village not far from ours. In fact she knew of our family because of the bakery and that they had attended the same church – they just hadn't met each other.

Slowly but surely we started to settle in and create a routine for ourselves.

Sleeping on straw mattresses was not so bad, though as it got colder we had to resort to using the heavy army blankets. After a while even they weren't enough, so we had to wear a jumper to bed as well. But we couldn't complain that we wanted our feather doonas like at home.

'Listen here, children', said Mum. 'Do not complain. Remember this: never again in your life will you receive food and a roof over your head without having to work for it. Just look at all that we are being given for free. We need to be very grateful and value all that we are being given here.'

One day a small group of people from the Nazarene church in the nearby city of Linz came to visit us. This was a very pleasant surprise. They kindly gave us some money, which we decided together should be spent on a clock. We had no way of telling the time. It was unanimously decided that it would be best to buy a wristwatch that could be hung from the wall but also worn by Mum if she was going somewhere. Eventually Mum started travelling to Linz most Sundays to attend this church.

Another thing we needed before long was something that could be used as a bath. There were public showers that I really didn't like and that were eventually closed down for some reason. Mum was able to buy a wooden trough from a family that was leaving the hostel. She also bought a wood-fired stove that was bigger than our little pot-belly stove and that would allow her to heat water and even do some cooking. There's only so much mass-catering food you can eat. Elenka somehow heard that if you took the food you got from the kitchen to one of the local butchers, he would swap it for some cheaper cuts of meat and give the kitchen's food to his pigs. With that Mum was able to make her own soup and mashed potatoes, which never tasted better! We still ate mostly from the communal kitchen but could have Mum's cooking once in a while. As for the trough, we were able to create a space for it behind the wardrobe. With a sheet pinned up for privacy, and with water heated up on the stove, that became our bath.

Eventually we met another family from our home town. They had two boys, one of whom had been at school with Vlado. They became good friends and we would spend many hours with them exploring the hostel grounds and even beyond that.

On one Saturday morning the boys were playing together

when they found themselves in the Jewish barracks area. Because it was the Sabbath, one of the orthodox Jewish people asked the boys to help them by doing simple jobs that their faith wouldn't allow them to do for themselves. This meant tasks as simple as starting a fire in the stove or even just turning electric appliances on or off. This quickly became a routine from sunset every Friday night. The boys were paid a small amount of money in return for their efforts, or if the people didn't have money they would give the boys some tinned food like sardines or some fresh fruit. At the end of each 'shift' the boys would compare what they had been given and have a bit of a giggle about the tasks that they had been asked to do.

I started doing a job too, once in a while. The ladies in the hostel were asked to help out in the communal kitchen about once a month, doing things like cleaning potatoes. Sometimes I would go in Mum's place and sit down amongst a group of women to cut the eyes and any black spots out of the potatoes after they came out of the peeling machine. It was interesting to listen in to the conversation, with women complaining about their husbands and things like that. One time a lady was talking about how her husband was a womaniser, and one of the ladies said, 'We have to be careful what we say in front of this young girl'. But I learnt a lot from those conversations.

Another time Mum and I responded when some potato farmers came to the hostel looking for workers to help bring in their crop. We went out into a paddock and after a tractor had turned over the soil we would pick out the potatoes. You would have to work fast enough to finish your area before the tractor came around again. I remember there was one farmer who also owned a restaurant and he gave us a free meal as well as our wage.

There was one upheaval in the hostel around this time. A meeting was called of everybody who was staying in the hostel. The person in charge said that he had an announcement to make. He told us that everyone was to remove their name from the door of their room. It turned out that a woman and her three children had escaped from Yugoslavia against the will of her husband, and that he had arranged for the family to be kidnapped from their room and returned to the old country. The job of the kidnappers was made easier by the family name that was on their door. They now wanted us to remove those names to prevent something similar happening again. It was all a bit unsettling now that we were feeling so safe in our temporary home.

As time went on, we kids – the four of us plus the two boys we had met – got more confident in our explorations.

Outside the hostel was a major road, though it wasn't a busy road by today's standards. One day we decided that we would cross this road and see what we could find. We soon came to another road, which we followed and that took us to the edge of a forest and then into the forest. This became a great playground, where we could climb over fallen trees or swing from branches and play hide-and-seek or cowboys-and-Indians amongst the ferns. We'd never seen ferns before, but they made wonderful camouflage.

Asten Lager, 1957. From left to right: me, Vlado behind Branko, Mum and Elenka, all of us in donated clothes

Every time we went back to the forest we would go a little deeper. One day we came upon a clearing with lovely green grass. We found that if we sat there very quietly, eventually birds would come to skip around the grass and feed, and then perhaps a deer might come out of the wood to graze. We had never seen deer before either, so that was fascinating. All I wanted after that was to have my own Bambi. This was a time when I would remember the words Mum said to us often as children: 'Treasure this time in your life, as it may never happen again: having it so good, and not having to work for it'.

After we tired of the clearing we became braver still. We discovered a very narrow path that led out of the clearing on the other side. We walked and skipped and squealed along this path for I don't know how far, then finally could make out light coming through the trees. We emerged from the forest thinking we had found another clearing, but this time we were out of the forest altogether. With eyes widening, we took in the scene below us. We saw a street with people busily walking to and fro, some in traditional Austrian costumes, some riding bicycles, and even a horse-drawn vehicle rattling down the street. Wow, what a surprise! To our right, we could make out part of a large grey building with a courtyard in front of it. There was a steady flow of people entering this courtyard, where they joined a queue and slowly, one after another, entered the building.

'Shall we go down to see where those people are going?' I asked.

'Yeah, you bet.'

We shuffled down the hill, crossed the road and followed the other people into the courtyard. Entering the building through a huge, heavy wooden door we found ourselves in a large room. Every wall of the room was lined with bookshelves from the floor to the ceiling. So many books! Whatever this building was, we had found the library. In the centre of the room were a number of glass-top cabinets displaying a few open books. There was a guide in the room who was obviously giving a tour, but as he was speaking German we couldn't understand him, unfortunately. Still, we followed the group anyway, entering another large room that was the most magnificent thing we had ever seen. It was breathtakingly beautiful, with gold covering much of the walls and ceilings, and enormous murals in between. There was no furniture in the room, so we guessed it must have been a grand ballroom. We were led to another, even more magnificent, room with heavy velvet curtains and furniture and paintings befitting a king and queen. Room after room our eyes got wider and wider, as we took in the magnificence of this place. Finally we were taken down some stairs to some underground tunnels and what felt like a dungeon (but was actually a crypt). One of the crypt's walls was lined with human skulls and bones, which was very gruesome.

It must have taken us several hours to get through this place and by the time we emerged it was late afternoon.

'We'd better hurry home,' I said to the others, 'before Mum starts to worry and dispatches a search party.'

When we got back we couldn't wait to tell Mum what we'd seen.

'You must come and see this place,' we told her. 'It is out of this world.'

We felt like we had spent the afternoon in a fairy tale.

We did go back to this place several times, including taking Mum and others to see it. I later learnt that the village was called Sankt Florian (Saint Florian) and that this place was the St Florian Monastery, one of the oldest still operating monasteries in the world. It is also renowned as a masterpiece of Baroque architecture. The crypt with the skulls and bones is known as St Florian Ossuary, and it is also the tomb of Austrian composer Anton Bruckner.

We weren't able to play and explore all the time at Asten Lager. Because no one knew how long we were going to be there, it was decided that we should be going to school. A school operated within the hostel for younger kids, which included all of us except Vlado.

Most of the time school was very boring, but not because we didn't want to learn.

The worst part was that we really didn't know what was going on, mainly because the teachers only spoke German, or I suppose it was Austrian-German. There were some students who spoke this language but most of us spoke something different. I remember a Russian girl, a Hungarian boy, a Polish girl, plus of course Yugoslavs, who spoke Croation or Serbian or Slovak.

The other problem with school was that it wasn't really very demanding. There were some kids who had been going for a few years, but most were expected to leave within a year or two, so the teachers couldn't make any long-term plans with us. I think they saw their job as a stop-gap until we finally found a new home. We were asked to copy from the blackboard into our notebooks, and to read in Austrian, even though we didn't comprehend any of it. Every day we recited times tables for maths, but that was easier because we could do it in our own language.

As well as school, anyone who was hoping to migrate to an English-speaking country would go to English classes in the evening. Mum and all of us kids went to this, where we learnt from Mr Podhorski. Mr Podhorski was of Croatian origin but had learnt English in America, so he spoke with an American accent. For me the biggest challenge was that I was learning English and Austrian-German at the same time, and these languages share a few words or have similar-sounding words: Brot and bread, Butter and butter, Milch and milk, Mutter and mother. I'd become Arthur and Martha and I didn't know what I was.

I guess if one positive came out of school it was that we learnt to form friendships despite language barriers. I especially remember Maria, who was Serbian, so I could talk to her a bit. Maria's story touched me a little. She was one of many children in a very, very poor family in Yugoslavia. However, she had an aunt who had no children, so to give Maria a chance in life she was adopted by this aunt. She left her home and family behind to go with her aunt to a foreign land. This story always made me feel sad about her situation, although she always seemed to be okay.

Waiting for Dad

Of course, no matter how comfortable we became at Asten Lager we were still missing some of our family. Dad and Daro were still at home and Miro was still in jail. Mum was most worried about Dad, of course. Daro had stayed of his own choice and Miro obviously couldn't go anywhere. And then there was Mum's decision that if Dad could not join us we would go back to Yugoslavia, which she obviously didn't want to do.

About three months after we left Bački Petrovac, Daro decided that he would leave after all. He applied for a travel visa to Czechoslovakia and somehow, despite our defection, he was granted one. He caught the train just as we did and then left it when it stopped in Vienna. Rather than ask for asylum there, he came straight to Asten Lager. However, he knew he should report to the police if he wanted to stay in Austria or even apply to go somewhere else, so he reported to the police station in Linz. As we expected, and just as we had been, he was placed in a jail cell while they checked out his story.

This was all fine, except that 28 days went by and there was no sign of Daro at the hostel. Mum decided to investigate, so she travelled to Linz to find out what was going on. It turned out that the police had locked Daro up and basically forgotten about him. They hadn't even done the checks they were supposed to have done. Perhaps it was because he was in Linz and not Vienna, where more people seeking asylum tended to show up. Anyway, the red-faced police had no answer. It turned out that when the Interpol check had been carried out on Mum, they had checked the whole family. If the police had bothered to find this out, they could have issued Daro with a permit to stay and an ID card without putting him in jail at all.

In the end no harm was done. Daro seemed to have a good time in the jail, being a comedian as usual. And within a couple of days he joined us at the hostel.

One day a man – another refugee in the hostel – came to our room to talk to Mum. He was perhaps ten or fifteen years older than Mum and very well dressed, wearing a boater hat and swinging a walking stick by his side that was obviously just an accessory.

The man told Mum he said he had a proposal for her. He explained that as a single man who was no longer young, no country was interested in accepting him as a refugee – that his only option for getting out of Asten Lager and Austria was to get married.

'Would you agree to a mock marriage?' he asked Mum. 'We'll just pretend. You can help me get out of here and get yourself, with your children, to the country of your choice. Then we can just go our separate ways when we get to Australia or America or Canada or wherever.'

We overheard all of this conversation, including Mum politely declining.

'I am already married,' she explained, 'and if I cannot be reunited with my husband then we will return to our home country.'

'Well, I will give you some time to think about it,' he said.

'I'm sorry, but I don't need time to think about it.'

Mum seemed very sure of what she was saying, though I must admit that the thought did cross my mind: *What if she said yes?* It made me fearful, no matter how many times I reminded myself that Mum's religion would never allow her to marry another man, even if it was just pretending.

It turned out that my brothers and sisters felt the same way, so we decided to do something to discourage this person, especially after he came back more than once looking for Mum.

One afternoon we told him to come back in an hour or so. Vlado found a nail and knocked it into the door frame above the door. He then filled a can with water and sat it carefully on top of the door, it's handle over the nail. And now we waited. After a time there was a knock on the door. He's here!

'Come in,' we called out.

The door swung open and as it did the can of water tipped forward, its 'ammunition' pouring straight down towards the floor.

Our visitor jumped backward, just missing being drenched, and it was only at that moment that we realised that it wasn't Mum's suitor who had come to visit. It was the hostel's Catholic priest. It was only because this man was much younger than the other man that he was able to avoid a bath.

We didn't try to explain what we were doing and so just played dumb.

'How can we help you, Father?'

The priest had come to see Daro. It turned out that he had heard that the Catholics at Asten Lager were getting a better deal than the rest of us: they were getting money from the church, and gifts. Anyhow, on this occasion he decided it probably wasn't the best time to discuss things with Daro, so he went away.

The other man, the one who wanted to marry Mum, might not have got what he had coming to him, but he subsequently got the message one way or another and we didn't see him anymore.

Of course the last thing Mum intended to do was go off with someone else. She had only one thing on her mind, and that was finding a way for our father to join us in Austria.

She knew from Dad's letters that the original idea – that Dad would be granted an exit visa to join his family once we were out of the country – was never going to happen. He made many appeals to the Yugoslav government to be able to reunite with his family, but each was denied. He was told quite clearly that because he had failed to join the communists, and had then tried to escape, he would never be allowed to leave. They told him he would be watched and eventually even required to report to a police station every twenty-four hours, wherever he was. He was also very lonely living in our big house on his own – the house where once there had been so much noise and activity.

After a while Dad had had enough. He packed a suitcase and left Bački Petrovac behind. He travelled to meet his brother Dušan in Banat, in north-eastern Serbia, then went on to visit his youngest brother, Vladimir, and his sisters in Croatia. Every day he would report to the local police station wherever he was. He made his way to Ljubljana and rented a room with a middle-aged traffic policeman and his wife.

In the meantime, Mum was trying to see what she could do at her end to help him escape. As most of the people we met in the hostel were refugees from Yugoslavia, there were lots of interesting tales about the different ways they had defected. Whenever this topic came up, Mum made it known that she was looking for a way to help my Dad to escape in a safe way. Sadly, there were too many stories of people losing their life as they attempted to cross the Yugoslavia–Austrian border.

One day a couple of men came to visit Mum. Each was carrying a Bible, and they told Mum that they had connections to the border.

'For the right amount of money we can bring your husband over,' she was told. 'But we will need the money upfront.'

Mum was wary. Dad had already lost money to people who had promised to smuggle all of us across the border.

'You can trust us,' they told her, holding out their Bibles.

'I understand that you need some money to make this

happen,' Mum said. 'I'll give you half the money now and the rest when I see my husband standing in front of me.'

The men weren't happy with this. They insisted that Mum pay up front, but she stuck to her guns. Eventually they stopped coming and Mum said to us, 'Remember this, children: beware of people who are hiding behind the Bible'.

Mum told us a few times that if Dad could not cross the border safely then we would all have to go back. We hated this idea. After everything we had been through, we just had to find a way for Dad to get out.

Ljubica was my younger sister's friend and schoolmate. When her mother heard about our plight, she spoke to Mum and suggested she talk to her next door neighbour, whose name was George.

'George may be able to help you,' said Ljubica's mum. 'He knows of someone in Yugoslavia who can offer a safe and sure way to get across the border.'

Immediately Mum went to see George and told him our story. George was a tall, intimidating man and his response was not what she expected.

'Look here, woman,' George said. 'I don't know who you are, and for all I know you could be a snoop who wants to get my friends, the people who helped me, into trouble. Just go away. I don't trust anybody and I will do anything to protect those friends.'

Mum, of course, was not going to be discouraged this easily. No matter how uncomfortable George made her feel, she persisted with going to see him and appealing for his help, explaining over and over that she and her children would need to go back to Yugoslavia if her husband couldn't get out.

'The thought of going back to that country fills me with profound fear', she said. 'There is no future for my children there. But I will not leave my husband alone.'

At long last her persistence paid off and George buckled under the weight of Mum's relentless begging for his help.

'I will help you Mrs Vasic, but it is of utmost importance that you keep this as the biggest secret of your life,' said George. 'These friends of mine are border guards and if they were caught helping people to get across the border illegally, their lives would be totally ruined.'

He then explained to Mum how the scheme worked.

'I will need your husband's photo to send to my friends. I will write to them informing them that the man in the photo, by the name of Daniel Vasic, will come to their place to seek ointment for treatment of arthritis.'

My mother was then instructed to write a letter to Dad containing the address of the people he was to contact and instructing him to visit them and ask them for ointment for arthritis.

George explained that his friends work fast and that as soon as Dad contacted them they would get him across the border without delay.

Of course we children knew nothing about any of this discussion – it was all completely secret between George and Mum. So when George came across me outside one day and said, 'Young girl, would you take this envelope to the post box?'

I agreed without a thought. The post box was about a two-kilometre walk but I was happy to do that. I took the letter and told him I would just go back and get my scarf because it was a bit cool.

I went back to our room and told Mum what I was doing. She looked at the letter in my hand and said, 'I have to open that letter.'

'What are you talking about?' I said. 'You can't open someone else's letter.'

I could tell she didn't want to tell me anything, but I could also tell that she was serious. If Mum wanted to do something like this there must have been a good reason.

Somewhere from the back of my mind I recalled a trick I must have learnt from one of my brothers. It was a way of opening letters then resealing them so that they would not look tampered with.

'We need the iron,' I told Mum.

We had to work fast because I thought George was probably outside waiting to see me go. The trick was to place a wet cloth over the envelope then the hot iron over that. The steam would soften the seal, allowing the envelope to be opened. It worked perfectly. Mum removed the letter and read it, then seemed to relax.

'Thank God,' she said. 'It is exactly as he promised.'

She replaced the letter, this time placing a dry cloth over the envelope and ironing it again. It sealed perfectly. No one would know that it had been opened.

I grabbed my scarf and the letter and opened the door to

leave. And there, towering over me, was George.

'On second thoughts I think it would be better if I post this letter myself,' he said. He took the letter from me and examined it. Looking at Mum, he continued, 'If my friends suspect that the letter was interfered with in any way, the deal will be off.' He walked away.

Mum and I stared at each other with wide eyes and open mouths. 'That was close,' she said, dropping onto one of the beds.

With just the two of us in the room, Mum decided that she needed to confide in me. She told me about how George was helping her, and why she felt she had needed to check on him.

'You must keep this to yourself,' she said. 'No one knows about this except you, me and George.'

'I will keep it a secret,' I said. I didn't need to be told twice how risky this whole thing was.

When the shock of George's appearance at the door had abated, Mum started to breathe more easily. Finally she had found someone she could trust. Now we just had to wait for Dad.

One week went by. Then two. Mum had heard nothing from Dad. Not even a letter, which was very unusual. George also thought it was unusual, but he had heard nothing either. With each passing day Mum became more panicked, though she couldn't say anything to anyone but me. I tried to reassure her that there was probably a good reason for the silence and that we would hear something soon.

One night I was woken in the middle of the night by Elenka talking in her sleep, as she often did. Everybody else was fast asleep. After whispering to Elenka to be quiet, I lay in my bed staring at the ceiling, now fully awake. The silence was broken by the sound of our barracks' back door opening and closing with its characteristic swish-swoosh sound. *Who would be coming in at this time?* My mind went back to the meeting we had had about a family being kidnapped and the hair rose on the back of my neck.

I turned and sat on the edge of my bed. I heard heavy footsteps getting closer and closer, closer and closer. I didn't know what it was, but there was something about those footsteps that seemed familiar. They got closer still ... and then they stopped. Right outside our door!

I held my breath as there was a quiet knock on the door.

'Mum!' I called out, jumping down from the bed. 'Mum ... Dad is here!'

The unmistakeable sound of my father's voice saying something confirmed what I had already worked out: that Dad had arrived.

Mum awoke with a start, stood and walked quickly to the door. I could see her hands trembling as she tried to unlatch the lock while also searching for the light switch.

We were all awake now and Daro said, 'Don't open the door, Mum. You don't know who it is'.

But I was sure, and then we heard that familiar voice again. 'Don't be afraid. It's me.'

The door swung open and there was my father standing in front of us all. We looked at him with dumbfounded disbelief, which quickly turned to ecstasy. As Dad moved into the room, he put down his small suitcase and a bundle he held in the other hand while we clamoured to wrap him in hugs. His trousers were wet up to the knees, and he was a bit scratched.

But he was here, with us.

No one got any more sleep that night as Dad told us his story.

He told us how for weeks he had moved ever so slowly closer to the Austrian border. We already knew that he had been moving around from his letters, but his plan was never clear. Basically, he had stayed in different places for no more than about a week at a time, always reporting to the police, and always getting closer to the border, slowly enough that he didn't arouse suspicion.

He told us how he had missed us so much, and often found himself sitting in parks watching children play to remind him of us.

Dad was out when Mum's letter – the one giving him the address he should visit – was delivered to the place where he was staying in Ljubljana. When he arrived back that afternoon he could see the letter locked in a cabinet, but it so happened that his hosts had left that day for a few days holiday.

It was nearly a week before he was able to get the letter, and when he finally read it he packed his things and made his way to the address as soon as he could. There he was greeted by a very friendly lady and her husband. They had received George's letter with Dad's photo some time ago and had wondered why he hadn't arrived. Now they asked him inside.

Dad explained the delay, and also told them how he was under surveillance and needed to report to the police every day.

'Thank you for this information,' the lady said. 'You will stay with us for seven days. In that time you must not communicate with anyone, including your wife. We will see during that week whether anyone comes looking for you. If not, it would seem they have lost you and we can continue with our plan. But if the police do track you down, then unfortunately we won't be able to help you.'

Dad was worried that it was now two weeks since he had been able to write to Mum, but he had no choice.

The days went by and nobody came, so on the Saturday night Dad, two other men and two guides drove in a car out of the city and deep into the countryside. They reached a forest at the end of the road, after which they had to travel by foot.

The three men walked through the woods in the darkness for many hours, constantly stumbling over the undergrowth. The guides and the other two men were younger and fitter than Dad, but kindly paused whenever Dad needed to catch his breath, and they helped him climb steep hills. Dad said he would forever be grateful for their assistance and patience.

When they were about three hundred metres from the border, the guides were given the agreed fee by each of the men. In exchange the men were given enough Austrian money for a train ticket. Dad was told which train to catch to get to the village of Asten, from where he could get a taxi to the hostel.

'Follow this path,' one of the guides said. 'It will take you right across the border. You will reach a train station on the Austrian side. When you reach the station you must split up. Do not speak to each other in Serbian. There are Yugoslav undercover police hanging around the station, trying to catch escapees such as yourselves.'

The guards wished Dad and the other two men good luck, and when the three of them reached the station they went their separate ways. They would never see each other again.

The next day Dad went to church with Mum and there were plenty of surprised faces to greet him. He also met George later that day and was able to thank him for his assistance.

With the knowledge Mum and Daro had from Daro's experience getting refugee status, Dad travelled to Vienna a few days later and was immediately given permission to stay in Austria and provided with an ID card.

And that was it, for now at least. We were all safely in Austria (and Australia) and out of the reach of the Yugoslav government, with the exception of poor old Miro.

Part Three

Salzburg

Now that Dad was finally with us, we could look forward to finding a new home with some purpose. Because my older sisters were telling us that Australia was not a good place, and also because Mum had some relatives in Canada who could support an application for migration, Mum had already made one application to that country for herself and her four youngest children. If she succeeded, the plan was that Dad would follow us there after he eventually escaped Yugoslavia. Daro had been old enough to make an application in his own right and this had succeeded, but Mum's application as a 'single' mother was rejected. This meant that Daro had moved to Canada while we had continued to wait in Asten Lager, hoping we would eventually be able to join him.

With Dad's arrival it was decided that a fresh application would be made to Canada. However, there was a hold-up due to a couple of health issues. Dad had had a severe hernia for a long time, along with a heart murmur, and he and Mum knew these could be a problem in applications to migrate to countries like Canada and Australia. In those times there wasn't much that could be done about the heart condition. It had kept him out of the army when he was younger, and it limited his fitness, but it didn't seriously affect his lifestyle. The hernia, on the other hand, was something he had chosen to live with – with great discomfort – because he was afraid of the idea of surgery. For years he had simply worn a belt for support, but it was very uncomfortable, especially with his work involving a lot of lifting. Finally, in Austria he was convinced to have the surgery because without it he would probably jeopardise our migration applications. He had the operation and recovered quite quickly ... then said it was the best thing he had ever done and regretted not having it sooner.

With that, Mum and Dad made a new application to migrate to Canada, but once again they were rejected, this time because of Dad's heart condition. With the United States being quite selective about who they would accept, we were really left only with Australia as an option, especially as the three older girls, all now married, were able to offer guarantees on our behalf that we would not be a burden on the government. When Mum and Dad applied to Australia, we were accepted. It was now a case of waiting for space on a boat that could take us there.

Around the same time that all this was going on – mid-1959 – Asten Lager was slowly starting to close down. Many of those who had been sent to the hostel had now moved on to new homes in other countries. Eventually it was decided that those of us who remained would be moved to another facility in Salzburg while we awaited passage to wherever we were going.

The Salzburg hostel wasn't really a hostel. It wasn't a

barracks, though it was an army base. Rather than having separate rooms, we were accommodated in large halls with panels separating family spaces. The panels had gaps at the top and bottom which meant you could hear everything that was going on in other people's 'rooms'. It wasn't ideal, but at least we knew we wouldn't be there for too long.

One of the first things we noticed about Salzburg were the surrounding alps. Bački Petrovac was in a very flat part of Serbia, and Asten was in a very flat part of Austria, so we had never seen mountains like this before. One time all of us kids did some exploring, climbing as high as we could up one of the nearby hills. I remember feeling giddy as we got so high that the air started to thin.

Mum and I got a job in a dry cleaner's, mostly folding washing. There was a nice lady in the shop – the mother of the owner – who spoke Czech, which is similar to Slovak, so we were able to communicate with her. Unfortunately her son was not a good employer, often aggressive. One of the ladies we worked with also lived in our hostel, a few rooms down from ours. Because of the open walls we often heard her husband abusing her, and her screams in response. There was a time when Mum plucked up the courage to interrupt them. She found this lady across her husband's knee being spanked like a child. Mum asked what he was doing and it was the silliest thing. All of us used to buy these bottles of *feferoni*, a type of hot chilli preserved in a type of vinaigrette. This man was drinking this very spicy preserving liquid and wanted his wife to do the same for some reason, but she was refusing. He was practically force feeding her. We also knew, from overhearing their arguments, that this man was always accusing his wife of having affairs – presumably at the dry cleaner's, which would have been difficult! Later we would hear much more about all this from the lady when we were at work. She also told us she was planning to leave her husband as soon as they got to America, which was where they were heading. Anyway, on this occasion when Mum interrupted them she gave the husband a bit of a lecture, telling him that after eight years of marriage it was time they trusted each other and that this was not the way couples should live. For some reason the man didn't tell Mum to mind her own business or to go away. I distinctly remember all this giving me an important lesson about relationships – that a couple doesn't automatically love each other as my parents had seemed to do.

Probably the best thing about our time in Salzburg was the English lessons I was given. The teacher we had had in Asten Lager was not very effective, just teaching us a few words like 'table' and 'floor', and a few basic sentences. This new teacher used written words with pictures, stories and games, including role plays like pretend shopping. I learnt much more in the six months with him than I did in the nearly two years we had in Asten Lager. Unfortunately, in the end I came to hate this teacher after he rubbished my father. He learnt that my mother tongue was Slovak, and then we met at the bus stop one day. He proceeded to tell me that my father was a 'chicken' because he had allowed his wife to convert him away from Serbian and the Orthodox Church and to raise his children speaking Slovak. I was glad this happened near the end of our time in Salzburg, as I didn't have to put up with this teacher for very long after he insulted my father like this.

We weren't in Salzburg for long before we started to plan for moving to Australia, including collecting goods to take with us. My older sisters had told Mum in their letters that we should bring enamel cookware, as they were cooking in aluminium pots (this was before stainless steel was widely available). We should also bring stainless steel cutlery because they couldn't buy good cutlery in Australia, and meat mincing machines, which they were also having trouble finding. They also wanted fabrics and clothes. Gradually we filled three large trunks full of stuff to take to the other side of the world. At one point we bought so much in one store that we were able to get a nice dinner set as a gift. The trunks were eventually sent away on a truck, after which they were shipped to Australia on a cargo ship ahead of us.

TN *Sydney*, the identical sister ship to the *TN Roma* on which we travelled to Australia. The *Sydney* also brought migrants from Europe to Australia

Australia

After about six months in Salzburg, the day came when we were to start our journey to Australia. It would be a long voyage.

We took an overnight train from Salzburg, which took us all the way to Genoa in Italy. There, we boarded the ship *TN Roma* that would take us all the way to Australia. The trip would take twenty-eight days. Tired from the train journey, we all slept so well in our cabin that we nearly missed breakfast the next day.

Our voyage took us through the Suez Canal and then across the Indian Ocean. It was fairly uneventful, with us kids spending our time exploring the ship from one end to the other, just making sure we were in the dining room on time for our meals. Mum and Dad spent a lot of their time outside at the front or back of the boat. They loved to watch the dolphins that often swam alongside us, seeming at times to be leading the way. We met quite a few fellow Yugoslavs, some of whom we would keep in touch with in Australia for many years.

Our first contact with Australian soil was when the *Roma* docked in Fremantle, Western Australia. We were able to leave the ship – there was a photographer at the end of the gangway taking pictures of everyone as they left – and we had time to wander around Fremantle for a while. It was all very strange to us. We walked through a shopping arcade and then came out onto a street lined with weatherboard houses. We had never seen wooden houses before. There was a wallaby in someone's garden which was amazing – it was just like the movies we had been shown of Australia back in Salzburg.

At one point we crossed a street and Mum noticed a half-eaten sandwich in the gutter. 'This is no good', she said. 'They have abundance here and they don't value it, throwing food away.' We would never have wasted food this way, and still to this day I have trouble with people who do so.

We didn't wander too far because we didn't want to get lost and have the ship leave without us. After a little while we returned to the boat and soon the journey continued towards Melbourne.

Me disembarking in Fremantle

Mum disembarking in Fremantle

I don't know how long that last leg of the trip took, but I do remember it was very rough for a while. There were enormous waves, unlike anything we'd seen before, some of them crashing over the deck.

Finally we arrived in Melbourne, travelling up Port Phillip Bay and docking at Station Pier in Port Melbourne. It was December 1, 1959; I was fifteen years old. There was a lot of excitement, with everyone gathering on the one side of the boat to try and see their relatives in the huge crowd below. I saw my sisters in the crowd and waved to them. But then it took ages to disembark. There were thousands of us with our luggage. But at least our journey was finished. Finally we were able to hug my sisters.

• • •

Although we spoke very little English, beginning a new life in Australia was not that difficult for us. Compared to life in a refugee hostel, Australia was like paradise. And we had my sisters here to help us find our way.

The first thing we had to get used to was Christmas. We saw it straight away, with decorations in the streets and in all the shops. Back in Yugoslavia the celebration of Christmas had been banned: you were not allowed to display a Christmas tree and carol singers were chased off the street. Here the celebrations were very open. And of course it was hot and dry, not cold and frosty.

Initially Elenka and I lived with Milinka and her husband Milan in the western suburbs of Melbourne, while the others stayed nearby with Ruženka, her husband Alfonz and her two-year-old son called Emil. (Veronka was living in Adelaide at this time. She had a nine-month-old son called Vladimir.) I learnt that I was old enough not to have to go to school in the new year (unlike Branko and Elenka), which was a huge weight off my mind. I was very worried about being embarrassed by my lack of English. However, that did mean that I was expected to join Mum, Dad and Vlado in trying to find a job. Unfortunately that task was made harder because of the time of year, with many industries closing down for summer and most not reopening until early February. We registered with the government employment office and were at least able to apply for the unemployment benefit until we could find some work. As it turned out, before we were paid any unemployment benefit we were offered some seasonal hop-picking work in the country town of Wangaratta. We were familiar with this job, as Mum had sometimes done it back in the old country. It was still school holidays, which meant Branko and Elenka could join us. So five of us – Mum, Vlado, me and those two – all travelled to Wangaratta by train and bus. Dad did not come with us, instead staying in Melbourne looking for longer-term work.

In Wangaratta we were provided with basic accommodation in shacks with portable beds and an outdoor barbecue for the cooking of meals. The work itself was not difficult but wasn't pleasant either. The hop plant has small thorns that scratch and cause a burning sensation on the skin, especially when you wash your hands. The hops also stain your hands and clothes a dirty brown colour – stains that cannot be washed off. I remember Elenka complaining that this wasn't what we should have come to Australia for: to work on a farm, under the hot sun. But Mum would hear none of it. She constantly reminded us that we should be grateful and that we had come to Australia with nothing but our suitcases until our other belongings arrived. As we were paid by the weight of hops we picked, Mum made sure we were the first to start and the last to finish every day. We worked six days a week for the six weeks we were there. Each night we would return to our accommodation exhausted. The only thing we felt like eating was chicken noodle soup from a packet, with chips fried in a frying pan on the barbecue.

Soon Mum and Dad, through our combined efforts, had raised enough money to put a deposit on a block of land in

Altona North, which made us all proud.

As Dad looked for work he eventually had two options: a bakery in Yarraville or the Don Smallgoods factory, which was close to where we were living (and would live). He opted for the meatworks because it would allow him to live a 'normal' life instead of working overnight, as he had for so many years. We were a bit concerned about how he would adjust to working in a factory, having been self-employed for his whole life, but he loved it. 'I do my day's work, and when I knock off I am free of any business responsibilities,' he said.

It was a busy time after we returned from Wangaratta in early February 1960. Elenka and Branko started school, Milinka gave birth to her first child (another Anna!), and I started working for the Pelaco clothing manufacturer, a job that Milan had found for me. I was working on sewing machines hemming handkerchiefs, which was not a 'natural' job for me, as I had no experience in sewing. When I messed up the machines (which was quite often) the boss lady would be angry with me, but because of my limited English I didn't understand what she was saying. I left that job as soon as I could, doing some seasonal work for Smorgons, where peaches were processed and canned.

My next work was at the Astor radio and television factory in Richmond. By now my eldest sister Veronka had returned from Adelaide to Melbourne with her husband so that they could be near the rest of us. Through the employment office Veronka and I were interviewed for Astor. Veronka and her husband Peter came with me for support in the interview because of my lack of English, but when the interviewer asked me basic questions like my name and how old I was, I was able to answer without help. I remember Peter trying to step in and help and the interviewer stopping him. 'She's doing okay,' she said, which made me feel very pleased with myself. Both Veronka and I got jobs and I really I loved doing the work. It was quite easy: placing electronic parts onto circuit boards for products like car radios. At first it looked very complicated, but everything was colour coded and there was a plan to check if we were confused. The downside was that Veronka and I had to travel across Melbourne to get to the factory and the train ticket cost almost as much as I earned. Being under age (I was still only fifteen) I was only earning six or seven pounds a week. Another 'problem' was that it was hard to learn English properly because there were so many different nationalities working in the factory: Greeks, Italians, Poles, Yugoslavs and others. As none of these people spoke grammatically correct English, we all shared each other's bad habits.

After about a year in Australia we all pooled what money we had saved to help Mum and Dad build a house on their block in Altona North. This would become our family home for many years.

When I turned eighteen I decided that I wanted to become a nurse. However, it was quickly clear that without having finished high school and with limited English, general nursing wasn't going to be an option. I applied instead to train as a nursing aide and I was accepted to the school, as was my younger sister Elenka. I still didn't think my English was good enough, but they assured me that I would be okay and that I would be able to use a dictionary in the exams (though I couldn't see how I would have time to do that). In the very first test, at the end of the first week, we were asked, 'What is the neat appearance of the ward?' and I didn't even know what the 'ward' was. Eventually I found a Croatian–English dictionary and that helped both Elenka and me to get through the course, along with a lot of hard work. We would study many nights until two o'clock in the morning and both succeeded in graduating.

And so we slowly settled into life in Australia. The plan was that Daro would join us here from Canada, but that never happened. He had all his immigration papers organised but had an accident just before he was due to leave. That left him hospitalised and his journey postponed. After his recovery he ended up marrying, and as his new wife was not keen on moving to Australia they remained in Canada.

Miro was finally released from prison and national service. He married and had three children, his family emigrating to Australia in 1967, after which he and his wife had another three children.

This was the same year that my father's health deteriorated and he died at just fifty-seven years old, only eight years after starting this new life in Australia. It was the saddest time of my life. We all missed him desperately, especially my mother.

One day after Dad had died, Mum received an unexpected letter from the old country. It was from my Uncle Dužan, my father's brother. Mum exclaimed that the letter was in Uncle Dužan's own handwriting, which was an achievement, as he had always been illiterate – he had been ill as a child and missed most of his schooling. He told of how he had called to visit us in the bakery one time but the minute he entered the shop he knew something was wrong. It was so quiet, with no one to greet him, no sound of children's laughter. He was gripped by sadness, weeping as he walked through the house, which was empty except for a scattering of objects and books on the floor. He had no idea what had happened to our family, but it was obvious that we had gone. Uncle Dužan told Mum how he had picked one of the books up off the floor. Being illiterate, he had no idea what it was about. He took the book home and asked his daughter to read it to him. The book turned out to be the Bible. After his daughter had read from this book many times, Uncle Dužan decided to attend his local Nazarene congregation. When the Bible was read during the service, he would ask someone to help him find the right page, then trace the words of the reading with his finger. Uncle Dužan joined this church and finally, over many months, he learnt to read. With his daughter's further help he also learnt to write.

Reading this letter brought Mum tears of joy at Dužan's achievement.

The year after Dad died I married Kalman Sagi, to whom I would be married for forty-eight years before his passing in 2018.

Mum went on to live for many more years, finally passing away at the grand-old age of ninety-four.

Some years after we had arrived in Australia, Vlado, who by now was living in Laverton with a wife and young children, was woken by knocking on his front door at two o'clock in the morning. It was decades since our childhood experience of being woken by banging on the windows at a similar time, yet the memories of that time still haunted Vlado. He refused to open the door, even though the people making the noise identified themselves as the police. This made the police suspicious. Vlado and his family were terrified, but his refusal to open the door would cause Vlado a lot of trouble, even though it was quickly clear that the police had the wrong address.

Talking to Vlado later, I asked him why he hadn't let the police in. 'This is not Yugoslavia,' I said.

'I didn't believe them,' he said. 'I didn't believe them.'

It was a clear demonstration of how distrust in authority can linger. For similar reasons my mother never really trusted authorities, even after many years in Australia.

The scars of corrupt government do not fade.

I will forever be grateful to my parents. I will always respect and admire their courage in being willing to leave all their worldly possessions and their homeland, plunging themselves into an uncertain future in a strange foreign land in order to find a better life and freedom for their children.

Thank you, Mum and Dad. Because of your bravery and struggle, my children and my grandchildren live in this lucky country, a land of plenty.

www.ingramcontent.com/pod-product-compliance
Lightning Source LLC
Chambersburg PA
CBHW031422290426
44110CB00011B/492